Venturi, Rauch & Scott Brown

John Rauch, Denise Scott Brown,
Robert Venturi

Venturi, Rauch & Scott Brown

Bauten und Projekte   1959–1985   Works and Projects

A. Sanmartín (Hrsg.)

K Karl Krämer Verlag Stuttgart

Danksagungen

Robert Venturi, Denise Scott Brown, James Bradbury und Stephe Estock danke ich für die Unterstützung und Aufmerksamkeit bei der Zusammenstellung des Materials für dieses Buch.

Julia und Howard Wescott sowie Betsy und Orie Dudley danke ich für ihre Großzügigkeit und Gastfreundschaft während unseres Aufenthalts in den USA.

Adrian Lucchini danke ich für das Interesse und seine Bemühungen bei der Gestaltung dieser Seiten,

und Silvia Bastos, die die Texte sorgfältig redigiert hat, danke ich für ihr Vertrauen in unsere Arbeit und ihre Mithilfe.

Acknowledgements

I owe their help and attention to recolect the material for this edition to Robert Venturi, Denise Scott Brown, James Bradbury and Stephe Estock.

I owe their generourity and hospitality to Julia and Howard Wescott and to Betsy and Orie Dudley while we were in the United States.

I owe the interest and effort to interpret the content of these pages to Adrian Lucchini,

and to Silvia Bastos, who carefully rewieved the texts, I owe her the faith in our journey and in what is ours.

CIP-Kurztitelaufnahme der Deutschen Bibliothek
Sanmartín, A. (Hrsg.):
Venturi, Rauch & Scott Brown: Bauten und Projekte 1959–1985 / A. Sanmartín, (Hrsg.). [Übers. ins Dt.: Cornelia Berg-Brandl].
– Stuttgart: Krämer, 1986.
ISBN 3-7828-1114-3

© Editorial Gustavo Gili, S.A., Barcelona, 1986

© **Karl Krämer Verlag Stuttgart 1986** (für die deutsche Ausgabe)
Alle Rechte vorbehalten. All rights reserved.
Übersetzung ins Deutsche: Cornelia Berg-Brandl
Printed in Spain
ISBN 3-7828-1114-3

Inhalt

Einführung
Vielfalt, Relevanz und Darstellung im Historismus, oder plus ça change… darüber hinaus ein Plädoyer für ein Muster in der gesamten Architektur, von *Robert Venturi* ... 7
Haus am Meer; Projekt ... 18
Haus Pearson; Projekt ... 20
Umgestaltung des Duke House ... 22
Verwaltungszentrale der Krankenschwesternvereinigung North Pennsylvania ... 24
Wettbewerb für ein F.D.R. Denkmal ... 28
Umbau Grand's Restaurant ... 30
Guild House ... 32
Haus Vanna Venturi ... 38
Brunnen in Philadelphia ... 48
Umbau der St. Francis de Sales-Kirche ... 50
National College Hall of Fame, Wettbewerb ... 52
Städtisches Verwaltungszentrum in Thousand Oaks, Wettbewerb ... 54
Fakultätsclub, Pennsylvania State University ... 56
Haus Lieb ... 60
Mathematische Fakultät, Yale University, Wettbewerb ... 64
Franklin Court ... 66
Haus Hersey, Projekt ... 68
Haus D'Agostino, Projekt ... 70
Trubek-Wislocki Häuser ... 72
Haus Brant ... 78
Umbau des Allen Memorial Art Museum ... 86
Tuckers Town Haus ... 94
Institut für Wissenschaftliche Information, Corporate Headquarter ... 96
Dixwell Feuerwache ... 98
Haus in New Castle ... 102
Western Plaza ... 104
Ausstellungshalle für Produkte der Firma Best ... 108
Museum für Kunsthandwerk, Wettbewerb ... 112
Haus in Vail ... 114
Hennepin Avenue ... 118
Gordon Wu Hall ... 120
Gebäude für Molekularbiologie, Princeton University ... 126
Staatsmoschee, Bagdad ... 128
Westway Park, Projekt ... 132
Ponte dell'Accademia ... 136
Alessi Teeservice ... 138
Sekretäre für ARC International ... 138
Möbelentwurf für Knoll International ... 139

Arbeiten und Projekte ... 141
Biographien ... 142
Bibliographie, auszugsweise ... 142

Contents

Introduction
Diversity, relevance and representation in historicism, or plus ça change...plus a plea for pattern all over architecture, by *Robert Venturi* ... 7
House at the Sea. Project ... 18
Pearson House. Project ... 20
Duke House Renovation ... 22
Headquarters Building of the North Pennsylvania Nurse Association ... 24
F. D. R. Memorial Competition ... 28
Grand's Restaurant Renovation ... 30
Guild House ... 32
Vanna Venturi House ... 38
Fountain in Philadelphia ... 48
Renovation of St. Francis de Sales Church ... 50
National College Hall Fame Competition ... 52
Thousand Oaks Civic Center Competition ... 54
Faculty Club, Pennsylvania State University ... 56
Lieb House ... 60
Hersey House. Project ... 64
D'Agostino House. Project ... 66
Yale Mathematics Building Competition ... 68
Trubek-Wislocki Houses ... 70
Franklin Court ... 76
Brant House ... 78
Renovation of Allen Memorial Art Museum ... 86
Tuckers Town House ... 94
Institute for Scientific Information, Corporate Headquarter ... 96
Dixwell Fire Station ... 98
House in New Castle ... 102
Western Plaza ... 104
Best Products Catalog Showroom ... 108
Museum fur Kunsthandwerk (Decorative Arts) Competition ... 112
House in Vail ... 114
Hennepin Avenue Transit ... 118
Gordon Wu Hall ... 120
Molecular Biology Building, Princeton University ... 126
State Mosque, Baghdad ... 128
Westway Park Project ... 132
Ponte Dell'Accademia, Venice Biennale 1985 ... 136
Alessi Tea Service ... 138
Bureaus for ARC International ... 138
Forniture Design for Knoll International ... 139

Works and Projects ... 141
Biographies ... 142
Bibliography ... 143

Einführung

Diese Monographie zeigt die unterschiedlichen Aspekte und Ziele des Büros von Venturi, Rauch & Scott Brown auf.

Auf den nachfolgenden Seiten werden Venturis theoretische und praktische Beiträge über ihre Bedeutung als Experiment hinaus – ob sie auf erfolgreichen oder wieder verworfenen Hypothesen beruhen – herausgestellt und der enge Zusammenhang zwischen Zeichnung, Konstruktion und Entwerfer aufgezeigt in dem Bemühen, eine endgültige Lösung für eine gestellte Aufgabe zu finden.

Jedem Objekt bzw. Entwurf ist eine kurze Erläuterung vorangestellt, die Venturi und seine Partner für Bauherren, Verleger und Kritiker verfaßt haben. Auf ihre Art sind diese Texte eher beschreibend als theoretisch. Sie geben eigentlich die leisen Töne wieder, die in der Arbeit eines Architekten wenig Beachtung finden. In der Übersetzung dieser Texte wurde versucht, den sehr persönlichen Stil soweit möglich durchklingen zu lassen. Die Texte, Zeichnungen und Objekte sollten nicht in einen größeren Zusammenhang gebracht werden, sondern stehen für sich alleine.

Die Projekte geben ihre Quellen, Bedeutungszusammenhänge, Ansprüche und Wirkungen offen wieder. Die grafischen Darstellungen, Zeichen, Objekte und Räume sollen aus einer »mittleren Distanz« betrachtet werden, und ihre konstruktive Definition artikuliert sich in einer Weise, die an Silben eines schweren prosaischen Gedichtes erinnern läßt.

Amerika, Venturis geographisches Umfeld, kann als ein allgemeiner Ort bezeichnet werden, ein Zusammenklang von notwendigen und überflüssigen Informationen, übertönt von tiefgreifenden, reinen oder aufrichtigen Werten, durchlässig für kulturelle Werke und befreit von der Last der Geschichte. Auf einem eine Quadratmeile großen asphaltierten Parkplatz, auf einem rechteckigen Stück Land außerhalb Philadelphias oder auf einem Bauplatz an der Ecke zweier verlassener rechtwinkliger Straßen für eine Feuerwache gibt es keine Geologie oder Geschichte. Und wenn eine solche Archäologie angetroffen wird, ist sie wohl zu offensichtlich. Aus diesem Grund werden trotz des intellektuell und in übertragenem Sinn gesehenen Kontext andere fremde Motive mit einbezogen, um eine eindeutige Abgrenzung und Konstruktion in der Architektur zu erreichen.

Das Architekturprogramm für die Gebäude und Projekte von Venturi, Rauch & Scott Brown – vor allem aus der jüngsten Zeit – gründet auf einer Reihe von Darstellungsqualitäten, die aus einer Realität herrühren, die schon eine fiktive Realität ist und sich den sozialen, urbanen, ökonomischen, ästhetischen, semantischen und sogar konstruktiven Verhaltensweisen anpaßt.

Ein solches Programm wird durch die Anwendung und Verwandlung der Formensprache, die dem Architekten eigen ist, und auf gewisse Art durch oft transzendierende methodologische Entwicklungsschritte oder durch a priori Konzepte erfüllt. Umrisse, Seitenansichten und industriell gefertigte Materialien sind Bedeutungsträger einer neuen, ersatzweisen, auf sich selbst bezogenen und konkreten Realität. Das ist so bei der Eingangsschwelle der Gorden Wu Hall, bei dem rot-weißen Steinmuster am Anbau des Oberlin Museums und bei den ausgeschnittenen Formica für die Knoll-Stühle.

Venturi und seine Partner verwandeln tiefgehende Aussagen in äußerliche Gegenstände, kondensieren die Dichte eines Raumes in den Eigenschaften des Materials und der Gestaltung der Oberfläche, bringen verschiedene Funktionen unter einem Dach zusammen und definieren das »Alltägliche« – das oft gar nicht so alltäglich ist – als eine wohlbekannte und eigenwillige Anspielung.

A. Sanmartin
Cambridge, März 1985

Introduction

The intention of this monograph is to present the diverse dimensions and purposes of the architectural practice of the firm Venturi, Rauch & Scott Brown.

The following pages, rather than presenting Venturi's theoretical and professional contribution as an exercise on successfull or abandoned hypotheses, intend to show the intense inquiry between drawing, construction and draftman in their search for the eventual solution to a given problem.

Every work or project in this catalogue is preceded by a brief explanation which Venturi and his partners prepared for clients, editors and critics. Seemingly naive, the texts are more descriptive than theoretical. Actually, they are the whispers left aside by the architect's making. Written in a highly personal style, they have been translated in an effort to retain as much as possible of the original tone. We have not attempted to develop a larger synthesis uniting texts, drawings and buildings but simply to let them stand by themselves.

The projects openly declare their references, intentions, components, assertions and effects. The graphics, signs, objects and spaces are to be perceived from a «mid-distance» and their constructive definition is articulated in a manner similar to the syllables of a difficult poem of prosaic content.

America, Venturi's geographical circumstance, can be said to be a generic place, a cacophony of necessary and redundant information deaf to profound, pure or transparent values, permeable to cultural achievements and freed from the weight of history. There is no geology or history in a 1 square mile asphalt parking lot, or in a rectangular piece of land outside Philadelphia, or in a site at the corner of two deserted perpendicular streets for a Fire Station. Furthermore, in occasions where such an archaeology can be found, it is likely to be too evident. And thus, although the context is intellectually and figurativly considered, other alien data are imported to achieve a complete definition and construction of their architecture.

The architectural program of the buildings and projects by Venturi, Rauch & Scott Brown, especially the most recent ones, is established by a set of representational qualities derived from a reality that is already a fictional reality shaped by social, urban, economic, aesthetic, semantic and even representation of the constructive procedures.

Such a program is solved through the adaptation and deformation of the architect's own grammar and in a manner often transcending methodological procedures or a priori conceptions. Silhouettes, profiles and industrial materials carry the meanings of a new, substitutive, selfreferential and concrete reality. This is the case of the threshold at the entrance of Gordon Wu Hall, the red and white stone pattern at the Oberlin Museum Addition, the reliefs attached to the concrete beams at the State Mosque in Bagdad and the Formica cutouts for the Knoll chairs.

Venturi and his partners turn «Profound» statements into superficial items, condense the depth of a space in the material qualities and composition of a surface, they shelter several functions under the same volume and interpret the «ordinary» —often not so ordinary— as a well-know and arbitrary reference.

A. Sanmartín
Cambridge, March, 1985

Vielfalt, Relevanz und Darstellung im Historismus, oder plus ça change... darüber hinaus ein Plädoyer für ein Vorbild in der gesamten Architektur

von **Robert Venturi**

Als ich jung war, war ein sicherer Weg, große Architekten zu erkennen, die Konsequenz und Originalität in ihrem Werk. Mies van der Rohe war bekannt durch seine unmißverständliche, sauber detaillierte Formensprache, Glas und Stahl, und verblendete Rahmen, die er generell anwandte, sei es bei Hochhäusern, Universitätslaboratorien oder den Häusern reicher Bauherren. Le Corbusier war herausragend durch *seine* spezielle Formensprache, kubistische Flächen in den frühen Jahren und monumentale, massige Formen in seinen späteren Jahren schweben zu lassen. Während beiden Perioden wandte er seine mehr oder weniger konsequente Formensprache auf alle Arten von Gebäuden an, sei es eine Kunstschule in Cambridge oder ein Haus in Chandigarh. Das gleiche gilt für das Werk von Frank Lloyd Wright, Louis Kahn oder Alvar Aalto (obwohl Aalto abweicht von seinen Kollegen durch seine Vorliebe für konventionell hergestellte Industrieelemente und deshalb durch sein Vermeiden von expressionistischer Originalität). Für diese Meister hätte eine Vielfalt von Stilrichtungen innerhalb ihres eigenen Werks Unentschiedenheit und das Fehlen von Bindung an ein allgemeingültiges Ideal bedeutet; doch das Gesamtwerk jedes einzelnen neigte dazu, sich zu unterscheiden von dem der anderen, da jeder danach strebte, eine Originalität zu erreichen, die als *sine qua non* künstlerischen Ausdrucks sowohl von romantischen als auch von modernen Künstlern verstanden wurde. Dies war eine Zeit in der Architektur, in der die Form über das Symbol erhoben wurde und allgemeine industrielle Entwicklungen überall als wesentliche Determinanten für die Form jeder Gebäudeart betrachtet wurden, so daß die Vorrangigkeit, die die ursprüngliche Formensprache des einzelnen Architekten hatte, eigenartigerweise verbunden war mit einem strengen Idealbild von formaler Einheit für die Architektur überhaupt.

Dies sollte nicht länger gelten. Lag die Stärke der modernen Meister in der

Diversity, relevance and representation in historicism, or plus ça change... plus a plea for pattern all over architecture...

By **Robert Venturi**

When I was young a sure way to distinguish great architects was through the consistency and originality of their work. Mies van der Rohe was known by his unmistakable vocabulary of finely detailed, glass and steel, veneered frames universally applied to high-rise buildings, university laboratories, or rich clients' houses. Le Corbusier was distinguished by *his* particular vocabulary of hovering Cubist planes in his early years and monumental statuesque forms in his later years. In each of these periods he applied his more or less consistent vocabulary to all kinds of buildings, whether an art school in Cambridge or a house in Chandigarh. The same could be said of the work of Frank Lloyd Wright, Louis Kahn or Alvar Aalto (although Aalto diverges from his peers in this respect in his tendency to work variations on conventional industrial elements and in his avoidance therefore, of expressionistic originality). For these masters varieties of style within their own *oeuvres* would have implied indecision and lack of commitment to a unified ideal, yet the work of each as a whole tended to look different from that of the others as each strove to assert the originality that was considered the *sine qua non* of artistic expression of Romantic and also of Modern artists. This was a time in architecture when form was emphasized over symbol and when universal industrial processes were considered essential determinants of form for all kinds of building everywhere, so that priority on the individual architect's original vocabulary was combined curiously with a rigid ideal of formal unity for architecture as a whole.

This should no longer be the case. Where the Modern masters' strength lay in consistency, ours should lie in diversity. But it still is the case. It shouldn't be because the Modern masters and what they stood for have been repudiated by current architects —often with a vengeance,

1. Kapelle Martorana, Palermo. Foto: Charles Brickbauer
2. Kapelle Pazzi, Florenz. Foto: Scala Istituto Fotografico Editoriale
3. Palazzo Rucellai, Florenz. Foto: Anderson
4. Palazzo Vidoni Caffarelli, Rom. Foto: Anderson
5. Maria della Piazza, Ancona. Foto: Stefani

1. Martorana Chapel, Palermo; Charles Brickbauer photo
2. Pazzi Chapel, Florence; Scale Istituto Fotografico Editoriale photo
3. Palazzo Rucellai, Florence; Anderson photo
4. Palazzo Vidoni Caffarelli, Rome; Anderson photo
5. Maria della Piazza, Ancona; Stefani photo

Einheitlichkeit, sollte unsere in der Vielfalt liegen. Aber es gilt noch immer. Es sollte nicht so sein, denn die modernen Meister, und das, wofür sie standen, sind von zeitgenössischen Architekten verworfen worden – leider oft mit bedauerlicher Heftigkeit – und jetzt suchen wir nach Inspirationen bei Architekten wie Sir Edwin Lutyens, der besonders in seiner Wohnungsbauarchitektur mit einer Vielfalt von historischen und dekorativen Stilelementen gearbeitet hat. Für seine verschiedenen Bauherren waren die Stilrichtungen, die er wählte, bedeutungsträchtig, und sie unterstrichen deren Positionen, sei es als Gutsbesitzer, weltlicher Kapitalist, Botschafter zu Washington oder Vizekönig in Delhi. Ich werde versuchen zu zeigen, daß ein Architekt sich heute eher durch Abwechslungsreichtum innerhalb seines Werkes und durch die Vielfalt seiner architektonischen Formensprache unterscheiden sollte, als durch Geschlossenheit seines Werkes und Einheitlichkeit und Originalität seiner Formensprache.

Vor etwa fünfzehn Jahren verfochten wir in *Komplexität und Widerspruch in der Architektur* und später in *Lernen von Las Vegas* architektonische Prinzipien, die damals als polemisch betrachtet wurden, heute aber allgemein als zutreffend gelten. Wir plädierten für eine Architektur, die Üppigkeit und Mehrdeutigkeit über Einheitlichkeit und Klarheit stellt, Widerspruch und Überfluß über Harmonie und Schlichtheit.

Unser Beispiel ist die Martorana Kapelle (1) – in deren byzantinischem Inneren strukturelle und räumliche Systeme von alles übergreifenden ornamentalen und bildnerischen Mosaiken, Fresken und Cosmatenarbeiten verdeckt werden, wodurch eine Vielfalt von Effekten erzielt wird. Wir wählen lieber dieses Beispiel, als das eines anderen, gern zitierten Archetypus, dem der Pazzi Kapelle (2), in deren Innerem einfache wesentliche Ornamente die Struktur und die Räumlichkeit unterstreichen, um so eine einheitliche Wirkung zu erzielen.

Eine solche Architektur läßt neben dem Dogma der Allgemeingültigkeit Raum für die Andeutungen eines örtlichen Kontext. Sie liefert eher pragmatische Lösungen realer Probleme als einfachem Gehorsam gegenüber idealen Formen – wie Stanislas von Moos es ausdrückte, sie löst Probleme, aber sie bringt sie auch zum Ausdruck. Bei einer solchen Architektur wird die dekorative Oberfläche der artikulierten Form vorgezogen, das Muster der Oberflächenstruktur und manchmal ein Muster, das alles überzieht. Die Architektur berücksichtigt wieder ihre grundlegenden Zwecke, Schutz zu bieten und Funktionen zu erfüllen. Und schließlich ist die Verwendung sowohl von Symbolen als auch von Raum und Licht ein Maß ihrer Kunst – sie erhält Bedeutung durch ihre Symbole und Ausdruck durch ihre Formen. Die Symbole, abhängig von Assoziationen, die ihre eigene Ausdruckskraft hervorrufen, fördern Elemente und eine Formensprache, die eher vertraut, alltäglich und konventionell sind als originell, fremdartig oder *avant-gardistisch*.

Diese Vorgehensweise vergrößert die Spanne der architektonischen Formensprache über die der industriellen, der vernakulären und der Maschinenästhetik des Internationalen Stils und das hi-tech der Spätmoderne, so daß sie also örtliche und kommerzielle Formensprachen und solche verschiedener historischer Stilrichtungen einschließt. Die Befreiung von der Einheitlichkeit und die Gelegenheit zur Vielfältigkeit, die daraus resultieren, sind wichtig: darin eingeschlossen sind ein Gespür für Ort, Zeit und Kultur und das Bewußtsein für die Verschiedenartigkeit und Relativität der Geschmäcker. Vielfältigkeit ist in der Tat verpflichtend, soll unsere Architektur nicht wieder eingeschränkt werden durch eine einzige, hochkulturelle Formensprache, von der erwartet wird, daß sie die Umgebung »abglättet« und »vereinheitlicht«, denn eine solche Formensprache tendiert dabei zu beschönigenden oder zu extravaganten Verzerrungen der ursprünglichen Ausdrucksweise, zur Degeneration oder zu einem langweiligen Aufguß der vorjährigen *Avant-Garde*.

Plus ça change...
Obwohl die meisten der oben genannten Prinzipien mittlerweile von

unfortunately— and we now look for inspiration to an architect like Sir Edwin Lutyens who especially in his domestic architecture worked in a variety of historical and decorative styles. The styles he chose were meaningful to his various clients and supported the roles they played as country squires, worldly capitalists, ambassadors to Washington, or viceroys in Delhi. I shall try to show that architects today should be distinguished by the rich variety of their work and the diversity of their architectural vocabularies rather than by the unity of their work and the consistency and originality of their vocabulary.

Some fifteen years ago in *Complexity and Contradiction in Architecture* and later in *Learning from Las Vegas* we advocated architectural principles which were then considered polemical but which are now accepted wisdom. We called for an architecture that promotes richness and ambiguity over unity and clarity, contradiction and redundancy over harmony and simplicity.

Our exemplar is the Martorana Chapel (1) —in whose Byzantine interior structural and spatial systems are obfuscated by an all-over applique of patterned and representational mosaics, frescoes, and Cosmati work, which achieve richness of effect. We choose this rather than another beloved archetype, the Pazzi Chapel (2), in whose interior simple integral ornament articulates structure and space to achieve unity of effect.

Such an architecture accommodates the intimations of local context over the dogma of universality. It provides pragmatic solutions to real problems rather than easy obedience to ideal forms —as Stanislas von Moos has put it, it solves problems, but expresses them too. It encourages ornamental surface over articulated form, pattern over texture, and sometimes pattern all over. This architecture acknowledges again the fundamental issues of shelter as well as function. And finally, it employs symbol as well as space and light as the measure of its art —it derives meaning from its symbols as well as expression from its form. The symbols, depending on association by their very nature, promote elements and vocabularies that are familiar, ordinary, or conventional rather than original, outlandish, or *avant-garde*.

This approach expands the range of the vocabularies of architecture beyond the industrial vernacular and machine esthetic of the International Style and the hi-tech of later Modernism, so that it can include local and commercial vernaculars and those of diverse historical styles. The freedom from consistency and the opportunity for diversity that result are important: inherent in them in sensitivity to place, time, and culture, and recognition of the multiplicity and relativity of tastes. Diversity is, indeed, an obligation if our architecture is not to be limited again by a single, high-culture vocabulary that is expected to «filter down» and «unify» the environment because such a vocabulary tends to degenerate in that process into prettified or extravagant travesties of the original vocabulary or into dry reditions of last year's *avant-garde*.

Plus ça change...
Although most of the principles catalogued above are by now a part of the accepted wisdom among architects and critics, nevertheless today's architects have achieved no more diversity or cultural relevance than their Modern forbears. It is this state of *plus ça change* that I shall deal with in this paper.

In the ever oscillating balance between form and symbol in architecture we are tilting at this time toward symbol. The trend toward symbolism is not surprising as it is a reaction to the long period when symbol was banned as a manifestation of ornament or historicism, or went unacknowledged, as was the case with early Modern industrial symbolism, or was substituted for by expressionistic articulation of structure and form, as in

Architekten und Kritikern als richtig akzeptiert werden, verfügen die heutigen Architekten nicht über mehr Vielfalt oder kulturelle Relevanz als ihre modernen Vorfahren. Es ist dieser Zustand des *plus ça change,* von dem meine Ausführungen handeln werden.

In dem ständigen Kopf-an-Kopf-Rennen zwischen Form und Symbol in der Architektur liegt zur Zeit das Symbol vorn. Dieser Trend zum Symbolismus ist nicht überraschend, ist er doch eine Reaktion auf den langen Zeitraum, als das Symbol als Manifestation des Ornaments oder des Historismus verbannt war, oder unerkannt verschwand wie im Fall der symbolträchtigen Industriearchitektur der frühen Moderne oder durch die expressionistische Hervorhebung von Struktur und Form, wie es in den späteren Jahren der Moderne geschah. Auf der anderen Seite erhebt sich jetzt, da wir die Zeichensprache in der Architektur wieder anerkennen, die Frage, was mit ihr zu tun ist. Für mich waren die Antworten bisher zu einfach, zu dogmatisch – ja es fehlte ihnen an Komplexität und Widerspruch.

Architekten haben sich herkömmlicherweise der Symbolik in der Architektur bedient, um deren Inhalte zu bereichern und um andere Aspekte mit einzubeziehen, einige fast wörtlich, die aus der Architektur ein nicht rein räumliches Medium machen. Symbolik dehnt die Reichweite der Architektur aus, um Bedeutung und Ausdruck einzubeziehen und einen klaren Zusammenhang zu fördern, sowohl denotativer als auch konnotativer Art. (Leider hieß das schon immer, daß schlechte Architekten prätentiösen symbolischen Schmus und bombastische expressionistische Strukturen entwerfen können.)

Vielfalt

Ein wesentlicher Grund, die Symbolik heute anzuwenden, ist, daß sie eine Vielfalt von architektonischen Ausdrucksmöglichkeiten bietet, den Verschiedenartigkeiten der Aufgaben entsprechend und empfänglich für die Eigenschaften des architektonischen Erbes und des Ortes. Diese Anwendung entspricht dem Bedürfnis, in unserer Zeit sowohl auf die Massenkultur als auch auf die pluralistischen Ausdrucksweisen zu reagieren. Die Welt ist heute zugleich kleiner und verschiedenartiger, mehr voneinander abhängig und dennoch nationalistischer; selbst kleine Gemeinden pflegen ernsthaft ihre ethnische Identität und zeichnen sorgsam ihre lokale Geschichte auf. Die Menschen sind sich heute ihrer Unterschiede bewußter, stehen diesen Unterschieden aber dennoch toleranter gegenüber.

Auch liegt in der Architektur zur Zeit der Schwerpunkt eher auf dem Einzigartigen als auf dem Allgemeingültigen. Die frühe Moderne wurde als Internationaler Stil bezeichnet, um gegenüber anderen Bewegungen ihre Allgemeingültigkeit zu proklamieren. Unsere Annäherung an die Symbolik, in unterschiedlicher Weise vollzogen, wird unsere Architektur von der unserer letzten Vorgänger unterscheiden, deren Gebäude wie Fabriken aussehen oder zumindest industrielle Bezüge enthalten mußten und so eine allgemeingültige industrielle Formensprache entwarfen. Aber die Art, in der wir uns der Symbolik bedienen, sollte unsere Architektur auch von der aus anderen Epochen unterscheiden. Wir können uns nicht, wie Architekten der Renaissance, der Geschichte bedienen, um einen einzelnen architektonischen Stil wieder auferstehen zu lassen; sie hatten eine homogene Kultur im Rücken, die weitestgehend einem humanistischen Erbe verpflichtet war. Ebensowenig können wir den Eklektizismus des 19. Jahrhunderts und die Kämpfe innerhalb der Stilrichtungen wiederbeleben, wie zum Beispiel den Kampf zwischen der englischen Spätgotik und der Hochgotik, die von der Oxforder beziehungsweise der Cambridger Bewegung vertreten und von jedem als einzige Ausdrucksform der kirchlichen Dogmen gefördert wurde. Unser Historismus sollte weniger eine Rivalität, sondern ein Konglomerat der Stilrichtungen sein; wie der freie Eklektizismus in den Gartenpavillons des späten 18. Jahrhunderts – gotisch *und/oder* griechisch –, der eine Vielfalt von historischen Assoziationen und romantischen Launen wachrief, oder wie die Architektur des 19. Jahrhunderts, in der geistreiche Verbindungen von Stilrichtungen die Funktionen und den Kontext einzelner Gebäude widerspiegelten.

the later years of the Modern movement. On the other hand, now that we again acknowledge symbolism in architecture, the problem becomes what to do with it. For me the answers so far have been too simple, too dogmatic —yes, they have lacked complexity and contradiction.

Architects have traditionally used symbolism in architecture to enrich its content and to include other dimensions, some almost literary, which make architecture a not purely spatial medium. Symbolism expands the scope of architecture to include meaning as well as expression, and promote explicit communication, denotative as well as connotative. (Unfortunalety this has always meant that bad architecture can project pretentious symbolic ballyhoo as well as bombastic structural expressionism.)

Diversity

An essential reason for using symbolism today is that it can provide a diversity of architectural vocabularies appropriate for a plurality of tastes and sensitive to qualities of heritage and place. This use suits the need to respond in our time to both mass culture and pluralist expression. Today the world is at once smaller and more diverse, more interdependent yet more nationalistic; even small communities seriously maintain ethnic identities and carefully record local history. People are now more aware of the differences among themselves yet more tolerant of these differences.

It's a time in architecture too when the shifting balance between the universal and the unique favors the latter. The early Modern movement was named the International Style to proclaim among other things its universality. Our diversified approach to symbolism will distinguish our architecture from that of our recent predecessors whose buildings had to look like factories, or at least contain industrial references, and promote thereby a universal industrial order. But our approach to symbolism should distinguish our architecture from that of other eras too. We are not able to use historicism, as did architecs of the Renaissance, to institute a rebirth of a single architectural style; they were backed by a homogeneous culture that was broadly committed to a humanist heritage. Nor can we revive 19th century Revivalism and the battles of the styles, like for example the battle between Perpendicular and Decorated Gothic advocated by the Oxford and Cambridge Movements respectively, and promoted as the exclusive expression of the ecclesiastical dogmas of each. Our historicism should involve less a rivalry and more a medley of styles; like the free eclecticism of late 18th century garden pavilions —Gothic *and/or* Greek— that evoked a variety of historical associations and Romantic moods, or like late 19th century architecture where dextrous combinations of styles reflected the functions and contexts of individual buildings.

In recent architecture historicism has been the major manifestation of the new symbolism. But it is important to acknowledge other sources of symbolism, including high-art and Pop —Scarlati *and* the Beatles— if diversity is to be achieved. In the design of individual houses our firm has adopted numerous local and vernacular vocabularies— more or less rustic or Classical. In our exhibition for the Smithsonian Institution we acknowledged the symbolic bases for American developer housing and studied the vernacular appliques these houses accrete over time as they are renovated, expanded, and ornamented by their owners. In *Learning from Las Vegas* we analyzed commercial vernacular vocabularies of the highway environment and urban sprawl, in a search for an appropriate symbolic architecture for our time. In the same book we discussed the machine esthetic of the Modern movement as a set of symbols rather than as a set of forms deriving from industrial processes of the modern world.

Another vehicle for symbolism in architecture is ornamental pattern. Ornamental pattern is different from historical, vernacular or Pop symbo-

In der jüngsten Architektur verwendet die neue Zeichensprache vor allem historische Elemente. Es ist aber wichtig, auch andere Quellen der Symbolik anzuerkennen, einschließlich hoher Kunst und Pop – Scarlatti *und* die Beatles –, wenn Vielfalt erreicht werden soll. Unser Büro hat beim Entwurf verschiedener Häuser ortstypische Ausdrucksformen aufgegriffen – mehr oder weniger rustikal oder klassisch. In unserer Ausstellung für das Smithonian Institut gingen wir vom amerikanischen Einheitshaus aus wie es von Baugesellschaften entwickelt wurde und untersuchten die ortstypischen Anbauten, die diese Häuser, wenn sie von ihren Besitzern renoviert, erweitert oder geschmückt werden, im Laufe der Jahre erhalten hatten. In *Lernen von Las Vegas* analysierten wir die ortstypischen kommerziellen Formensprachen in Gegenden nahe der Landstraße und in städtischen Komplexen auf der Suche nach einer angemessenen Zeichensprache für die Architektur unserer Zeit. Im selben Buch bezeichneten wir die Maschinenästhetik der Moderne als eine Sammlung von Symbolen und nicht als eine Formensprache, die aus industriellen Prozessen der modernen Welt entstanden ist.

Ein anderer Träger für Symbolik in der Architektur ist das Ornament. Das Ornament unterscheidet sich von historischer, vernakulärer oder Pop-Symbolik, indem es freier und weniger konsequent sein und weniger von Assoziationen abhängen kann. Es kann heute für die Architektur sehr bedeutsam sein und bietet ein enormes Potential zur Weiterentwicklung. Ich werde später darauf zurückkommen.

Relevanz

Architektur kann viele Bedeutungen haben, aber sie sollte zweckdienlich sein. Wie Denise Scott Brown hervorgehoben hat (1), sollte sie kulturell relevant sein. Es ist notwendig, diesen offenkundigen Aspekt herauszustellen, denn in der heutigen Architektur ist die Symbolik häufig willkürlich. Architekten, die ihrer Vorliebe für esoterische und exotische Symbole frönen, neigen dazu, eine Architektur wunderlicher Pavillons und pittoresker Verrücktheiten zu machen, die den Unterschiedlichkeiten und geschmacklichen Feinheiten der jeweiligen Kulturen oder dem umgebenden Kontext, der doch der Form Substanz geben sollte, nicht genügend entspricht. Angemessenheit sollte sich aber nicht nur auf die unterschiedlichen Kulturformen beziehen, sondern auch auf die Hierarchie kultureller Werte – nicht alle Gebäude sind gleichermaßen bedeutend, nicht alle Gebäude sollten große Kunstwerke sein, in den meisten Landschaften sollte es schlichte wie außergewöhnliche Gebäude geben.

Bei dem Versuch, eine Architektur zu entwickeln, die die Unterschiedlichkeiten von Kultur, Geschmack und Ort berücksichtigt, legte ich mehr Gewicht auf die Symbolik als auf die formalen und technischen Gesichtspunkte der Architektur. Der Grund dafür ist, daß symbolische Elemente flexibler und leichter anwendbar sind als formale und besonders als konstruktive Elemente. Auch unterliegen sie weniger irgendwelchen Einschränkungen durch Verwendung, Kosten und Material sowie Zwängen, die durch die Standardisierung entstehen. Bausysteme und die daraus resultierenden Formen sollten vielmehr allgemeingültige Qualitäten in unserer Architektur schaffen und als Kontrapunkt zu den einzigartigen Qualitäten fungieren, die Symbolcharakter haben werden. Für unsere Gebäude im Irak beispielsweise wählten wir eine Betonrahmenkonstruktion mit vorgefertigten Paneelen, eine überall übliche Bauweise. Einen Teil der Öffnungen in den vorgefertigten Paneelen bildeten wir jedoch als Spitzbögen aus, um den Wünschen unserer Bauherren entgegenzukommen, nationalen Charakter zu symbolisieren und das kulturelle Erbe in ihrer Architektur zum Ausdruck zu bringen.

In meinem Artikel »Architektur als dekorierte Hülle« habe ich mich für eine Trennung von Form und Symbol eingesetzt. Ich betonte dabei den Widerspruch zwischen Form und Funktion und deren Unterscheidung: Form und Funktion zu gestatten, getrennte Wege zu gehen, erlaubt der Funktion tatsächlich funktional zu sein – wie es, ironischerweise, nicht der Fall sein konnte, als in Zeiten der frühen Moderne die Form der Funktion folgte und dabei zugleich gut aussehen und funktionieren mußte.

lism in that it can be freer and less consistent and can depend less on association. It could be extremely significant for achitecture now and has enormous potential for development. I shall return to it later in this paper.

Relevance

Architecture can be many things, but it should be appropriate. As Denise Scott Brown has pointed out[1], it should have cultural relevance. It is necessary to make this obvious point because today's architecture is frequently arbitrary in its symbolism. Architects who indulge their preferences for esoteric and exotic symbols tend to produce architecture of whimsical pavilions and picturesque follies that makes insufficient reference to the diversities and subtleties of taste cultures at hand or to the context of place which should give substance to form. But a sense of appropriateness should apply not only to a variety of cultural types, but also to a hierarchy of cultural values —not all buildings are equally important, not all buildings should be high art, most landscapes should include buildings plain and fancy.

In attempting to derive an architecture that is relevant for diversities of culture, taste and place, I put the burden on the symbolic rather than the formal or technical aspects of architecture. This is because symbolic elements are more flexible and adaptable than formal and especially structural-technical elements. They are also less subject to limitations of use, cost, and physical stability and to the constraints of standardization. Building systems and their resultant forms should constitute the more universal qualities in our architecture and act as counterpoint to the unique qualities that will be symbolic. The construction method of our building in Iraq, for instance, is concrete frame with pre-cast panels which is standard world-over; yet some of the openings in the pre-cast panels we designed as pointed arches to conform to the desires of our clients to symbolize national character and express cultural heritage in their architecture.

I have made a case for a separation between form and symbol in the article «A Definition of Architecture as Shelter with Decoration on It». My emphasis there was on contradiction as well as separation between form and function: allowing form and function to go their separate ways permits function to be truly functional —as it couldn't be, ironically, when Form followed Function in the old Modern days, and had the obligation to look good as well as work well.

So the independence of form and function in the interest of more effective functionalism can distinguish our architecture from that tof the Modern movement. But the independence of form and symbol in the service of cultural relevance can distinguish it also from traditional historicist architecture. Renaissance buildings, for instance, were constructed more or less like the Roman buildings they emulated (although the Romans were more technically advanced in the use of concrete) while Revivalist buildings of the last two centuries were also almost identical in how they were constructed to the buildings they copied —Gothic, Classical, or Renaissance— give or take a few steel or cast iron members imbedded in the masonry. And the vernacular revivals of the turn of the century represented survivals more than revivals in that «arts and crafts» as a building tradition continued to exist. Building technology hadn't changed much until recently. In most eras contemporary form and historical symbol could be integral for the whole building; it is only our age that has seen grand contradictions between structure and symbol, or form and symbol.

Modern technical forms and historical symbolic forms rarely harmonize now. Historical symbolism and ornamental pattern must almost inevitably become applique. Quoins on the corner of a façade *could* be structural in a Renaissance or Revivalist façade even if they *were* applied; but not now, because we build differently. We see differently too. We

So kann die Unabhängigkeit von Form und Funktion im Interesse eines effektiveren Funktionalismus unsere Architektur von der der Moderne abheben. Aber die Unabhängigkeit von Form und Symbol im Dienste einer kulturellen Relevanz kann sie ebenso von der traditionellen historisierenden Architektur unterscheiden. Gebäude der Renaissance beispielsweise waren mehr oder weniger konstruiert wie die römischen Gebäude, denen sie nacheiferten (obwohl die Römer im Umgang mit dem Material technisch fortschrittlicher waren), während die eklektizistischen Gebäude der letzten Jahrhunderte von der Konstruktion her fast identisch waren mit denen, die sie kopierten – Gotik, Klassizistik oder Renaissance – abgesehen von ein paar Stahl- oder Gußeisenteilen im Mauerwerk. Und das lokale Wiederaufleben verschiedener Stile um die Jahrhundertwende bedeutete eher ein Überleben als ein Wiederaufleben, da nämlich das Kunstgewerbe als Bautradition gleichermaßen weiterexistierte. Die Bautechnologie hat sich bis vor kurzem kaum verändert. In den meisten Zeitaltern konnten zeitgenössische Formen und historische Symbole in einem Gebäude vereint werden; erst in der heutigen Zeit erkannte man die großen Widersprüche zwischen Konstruktion und Symbol, oder Form und Symbol.

Moderne technische Formen und historische symbolische Formen harmonieren heutzutage selten. Historische Symbole und Ornamente müssen zwangsweise fast immer aufgesetzt wirken. Fassadenecksteine *konnten* bei einer Renaissance- oder Gründerzeitfassade konstruktiv sein selbst wenn sie aufgesetzt *waren,* heute aber nicht mehr, denn wir bauen anders. Wir sehen auch anders. Wir *wollen* keine Harmonie zwischen Konstruktion und Symbol, wenn sie aufgezwungen und unecht ist. Wenn wir schließlich »postmodern« genug sind, bauliche und formale Widersprüche zu akzeptieren, sind wir immer noch »modern« genug, bauliche und formale »Unehrlichkeit« abzulehnen. Wenn wir die Konstruktion nicht zeigen müssen, wollen wir sie nicht verfälscht darstellen. Ein »trompe l'œuil« in der Architektur ist für uns nur dann wirklich, wenn er befreit ist von der Funktion.

Darstellung

Ich habe das Was und das Warum der Vielfalt und der Relevanz von Symbolen in der Architektur angesprochen, was die historisierende Symbolik betrifft. Ich will jetzt das Wie ansprechen und nenne dies die Darstellung in der Architektur, erreicht durch Abbildungen und Applikationen.

Die Unterscheidung von Fassade und Konstruktion durch die Hinzufügung von Paneelen auf oder innerhalb eines Rahmens ist uns aus der Architektur der Moderne vertraut. Als die nicht tragenden Wände oder die modulen Paneele bemalt oder oberflächenbehandelt wurden (sie waren selten gemustert), hatten sie einen quasi-dekorativen Effekt, was sonst selten war in dieser Architektur. Aber diese nicht-konstruktiven Mauern in der Moderne hatten vor allem eine räumliche Funktion – die Marmorscheiben, verteilt im Konstruktionsraster des Barcelona Pavillons geben dem fließenden Raum eine Richtung, und die gekurvten Mauern, die sich durch die Stützenfelder im Parlamentsgebäude von Chandigarh schlängeln, umschließen einen besonderen Raum, während der Modul der Paneele das Konstruktionsraster im gleichen Gebäude ergänzt. Ich habe mich statt dessen für die Verwendung von einem hinzugefügten Element als Zeichen eingesetzt, dessen Funktion nicht in erster Linie räumlich oder konstruktiv ist, sondern kommunikativ, und zwar mittels des Symbols und des Ornaments. Es ist diese Art der Anwendung, die unser hinzugefügtes Element von dem unserer jüngsten Vorgänger unterscheidet. Als lebendigster historischer Vorläufer für unsere Vorgehensweise kann wieder der Innenraum der Byzantinischen Kapelle dienen, in dem ein Fresko oder ein Mosaik ein aussagekräftiger Bedeutungsträger ist – symbolischer und darstellender Art – und von der Architektur inhaltlich und formal unabhängig ist. Der Inhalt ist religiös, die Form ist ein Bautyp und die Form und der Rhythmus haben nichts mit den räumlichen Elementen zu tun, die Aufteilung und der Rhythmus haben nichts zu tun mit den räumlichen oder konstruktiven Elementen, auf die sie aufgebracht sind. So kann der Kopf eines

don't *want* harmony between structure and symbol if it is forced or false. If we are at last «Post-modern» enough to accept structural and formal contradiction, we are still «Modern» enough to reject structural and formal «dishonesty». If we don't have to express structure, we don't want to falsify it. *Trompe l'oeuil* in architecture is effective for us only so far as it doesn't work.

Representation

I have been discussing the what and the why of diversity and relevance in architectural symbolism —as it applies to historicist symbolism. I will now discuss the how of the subject which I will characterize as representation in architecture. Representation in architecture achieved through depiction and applique.

The separation of wall and structure through the applique of panels on or within a frame is familiar to us in Modern architecture. When the independent walls or the modular panels were colored or textured (they were seldom patterned) they provided a quasi-ornamental effect, otherwise rare in that architecture. But these non-structural walls in Modern architecture were essentially spatial in function —the marble panels interspersed in the structural grid of the Barcelona Pavilion directed flowing space and the curving walls snaking through the bays of the Parliament in Chandigarh enclosed particular space while the modular panels complemented the structural grid in the same building. Instead, I have advocated the use of applique as sign, whose function is not basically spatial or structural, but communicative, via symbolism and ornament. It is this quality which distinguishes our applique from that of our recent predecessors. The most vivid historical precedent for our approach is again the interior of a Byzantine chapel where a fresco or mosaic applique communicates explicit messages —symbolic and representational— and is independent of the architecture in content and form. The content is religious, the form is pattern, and the configurations and rhythms have nothing to do with the spatial or structurations and rhythms have nothing to do with the spatial or structural elements they are applied to. The representation of a saint's head might be tilted forward on the curved surface of the ceiling vault while his feet might be amputated by an arched opening in the wall below.

In *Complexity and Contradiction in Architecture* I analyzed spatial layering and «things within things» exemplified by the pierced multiple domes of Baroque churches and other kinds of architectural juxtaposition involving redundancy. These complex forms of applique I opposed to the complicated, Piranesian and Paxtonesque spatial configurations that late Modern architecture had substituted for symbolism and ornament. In *Learning from Las Vegas* we analyzed commercial roadside building as one model for a symbolic architecture and illustrated our Football Hall of Fame Competition entry which we called a building-board. From these sign-appliques we developed the idea of the decorated shed as a building type and as a vehicle for ornament in architecture.

In the progression of our ideas about applique, first as spatial layerings, then signboard, and then ornament, we came to applique as representation in architecture. Representation in this context involves the *depiction* as opposed to the *construction* of symbol and ornament. Manifestations of this approach to symbolism in architecture are essentially two-dimensional and pictorial. Examples of representation in historicist architecture could be Classical columns or hammerbeam trusses cut out as silhouettes which depict but don't reconstruct the originals, or Classical quoins which are incised on a façade and which brook no ambiguity as to their symbolic and decorative function (3, 4). Much of the early work of Gunnar Asplund and of some other early 20th century architects espoused a non-literal historicism which was expressed through representatio-

heiligen durch die gebogene Oberfläche des Deckengewölbes nach vorne geneigt dargestellt sein, während seine Füße von einem Gewölbebogen der darunterliegenden Wand abgeschnitten werden können.

In *Komplexität und Widerspruch in der Architektur* analysierte ich die räumliche Schichtung und »Dinge in Dingen«* am Beispiel der zahlreichen Durchdringungen von Kuppeln in Barock-Kirchen und anderen architektonischen Elementen, die, nebeneinandergestellt, die Idee der Redundanz vermitteln. Ich stellte diese komplexen Formen der Applikation den komplizierten räumlichen Konfigurationen von Piranesi und Paxton gegenüber, in denen die jüngste Moderne einen Ersatz für Symbole und Ornamente fand. In *Lernen von Las Vegas* analysierten wir kommerzielle Straßenbebauung als ein Modell für eine symbolträchtige Architektur, und wir illustrierten dies mit unserem »Football Hall of Fame«-Wettbewerbsbeitrag, den wir als Gebäude-Anzeigetafel, ›building-board‹, bezeichneten. Von diesen aufgesetzten Zeichen ausgehend, entwickelten wir die Idee des dekorierten Schuppens als Gebäudetyp und als Träger für das Ornament in der Architektur.

In der Entwicklung unserer Idee über die Applikation, erst als räumliche Schichtung, dann als Zeichenträger und dann als Ornament, kamen wir zur Applikation als einer Möglichkeit der Darstellung in der Architektur. Darstellung in diesem Zusammenhang bedeutet die *Abbildung* im Gegensatz zu der *Konstruktion* von Symbol und Ornament. Die Wiedergabe dieser Auffassung vom Symbol in der Architektur ist im wesentlichen zweidimensional und bildhaft. Als Beispiele für die Darstellung in der historischen Architektur können die klassischen Säulen oder die Polygonaldachbinder dienen, die als Silhouetten ausgebildet sind, die die Originale darstellen, aber keine Rekonstruktion derselben sind, oder klassische Ecksteine, die in eine Fassade eingeritzt sind und die, was ihre symbolische und dekorative Funktion betrifft, keine Mehrdeutigkeit zulassen (3, 4). Ein großer Teil der frühen Arbeiten Gunnar Asplunds und einiger anderer Architekten des frühen 20. Jahrhunderts tritt für ein nicht wörtliches Zitieren des Historismus ein, der mittels Ornamenten zum Ausdruck gebracht wurde. In anderen, weniger historischen Ornamenten kann ein Blumenmuster beispielsweise eher auf normale Tapetenblumen denn auf echte Blumen anspielen; die zusätzliche Deutungsebene bereichert den Symbolwert.

Ornamente in der volkstümlichen Architektur zu verwenden heißt oft, repräsentative kunstvolle Ornamente zu vereinfachen und auf zwei Dimensionen zu verkürzen, sei es durch auf glatte Oberflächen gemalte Muster oder durch die Wirkung durchbrochener Formen. Beispiele dafür sind Tischlerarbeiten an amerikanischen Frontveranden oder die Bretterschnitzereien alpiner Balkonbrüstungen. Wirtschaftlichkeit und Naivität waren vermutlich die eigentlichen Gründe für diese repräsentative Handhabung, aber die ästhetischen Folgen waren eloquenter Ausdruck des Stilwesens. In der heutigen Zeit rechtfertigen die industrielle Standardisierung einerseits und das Fehlen von Handwerkskunst andererseits diese vereinfachte, sich dauernd wiederholende und darstellerische Handhabung des Ornaments.

Wenn wir heute historische Architektur nicht mehr konstruieren oder den Eklektizismus wiederbeleben können, so können wir diese doch mittels Applikation und Zeichen darstellen. Diese Techniken mögen einfältig erscheinen, aber sie können uns helfen, die Fehler schlechter Mehrdeutigkeit zu vermeiden und uns frei machen für die Schaffung einer für unsere Zeit guten Architektur.

Plus plus ça change

Der Begriff Postmoderne kommt, so glaube ich, aus Princeton, wo ich ihn zuerst von Jean Labatut hörte, der damit eine Architektur der mittvierziger Jahre beschrieb. Der Begriff wird heute überall großzügig angewandt, um jede Art von divergierenden architektonischen Trends zu bezeichnen. Er umfaßt zum Beispiel die italienische rationalistische Bewegung, obwohl diese Bewe-

* »things in things« (Anm. d. Übers.)

nal ornament. In other, less historical ornament, a flower pattern, for instance, may allude to conventional wallpaper flowers rather than to real flowers; the extra layer of meaning makes the symbolism richer.

Ornament in folk architecture is often representational highart ornament simplified and rendered in two dimensions through painted patterns on flat surfaces, or through silhouettes. The jig-saw carpentry of American front porches or the cut-out boards of Alpine ballustrades are examples. Economy and naivete were probably the immediate reasons for this representational approach, but its esthetic results were eloquent expressions of the essence of style. In our time, economy and industrial standarization on one hand and lack of craftsmanship on the other justify this simplified, repetitive, and depictive approach to ornament.

If we cannot construct historical architecture today or revive Revivalism, we can represent them through applique and sign. These techniques may seem simple-minded, but they can help us avoid the flaws of bad ambiguity and free us to create an architecture good for our time.

Plus plus ça change

The source of the term Post-modern I believe to be Princeton where I first heard Jean Labatut use it to describe and architecture in the mid-forties. The term is widely and loosely used today to cover ever-divergent architectural trends. It includes for example the Italian Rationalist movement, although that movement is an entity in itself and has in fact influenced the American Post-modern movement especially in its adoption of a Neo-classicist vocabulary.

My evaluation of Post-modernism will cover only the movement's approach to diversity, cultural relevance, and symbolism as I have been discussing them. My view will be limited by the bounds of my knowledge of current architecture and will be based more on the projects of Post-modernist architects than on their theoretical writings. I am in general in agreement with the theoretical bases of Post-modernism; the concurrent architecture and its apparent implications are what concern me.

Post-modernism has in my opinion proclaimed in theory its independence from Modernism —from the singular vocabulary and the rigid ideology of that movement— but has substituted, in practice, a new vocabulary that is different in its symbolism from that of the old, but similar in its singularity and as limited in its range and dogmatic in its principles as the old. The new movement does not provide the diverse symbolism and cultural relevance appropriate for our era. In this respect it is not different from the previous movement. *Plus ça change...*

The Post-modernists have abandoned the universal industrial vocabulary of Modernism. As wed said in *Learning from Las Vegas,* everyone but architects had come to know that the Industrial Revolution was dead and its continued glorification ironical. We pointed out that, although Le Corbusier's late-Modern *beton-brut* was symbolically anti-industrial, in the hands of his followers it had become expressionistically heroic and as irrelevant as the industrial vocabulary it replaced. However, the Post-modernists in supplanting the Modernists have substituted for the largely irrelevant universal vocabulary of heroic industrialism, another largely irrelevant universal vocabulary— that of parvenue Classicism, with, in its American manifestation, a dash of Deco and whiff of Ledoux. In substituting historical symbolism for Modern symbolism, they have promoted a kind of Neo-classicism, striving for a universalism which was appropriate at the turn of the 18th century to the aristocratic and republican patrons of Neo-classicism and to the essentially homogeneous preindustrial societies in which they lived, but which is inappropriate for post-industrial societies like ours which are complex and pluralist. In this context the architectural jumps of the 1970s from Le Corbusier to Ledoux, from Whites to pastels, were not such big leaps as they sound. The transition from the

gung in sich geschlossen ist und sogar die amerikanische Postmoderne beeinflußt hat, insbesondere in deren Anwendung der neo-klassizistischen Formensprache.

Meine Bewertung der Postmoderne beinhaltet nur deren Annäherung an die Vielfalt, die kulturelle Relevanz und die Symbolik, in dem Sinn, in dem ich mich darüber ausgelassen habe. Mein Blickwinkel ist begrenzt durch meine Kenntnisse von der derzeitigen Architektur und basiert mehr auf den Projekten von postmodernen Architekten als auf deren Theorien. Im allgemeinen stimme ich mit den theoretischen Grundlagen der Postmoderne überein; es ist die entsprechende Architektur und deren augenscheinliche Auswirkung, die mich angeht.

Die Postmoderne hat meiner Meinung nach in der Theorie ihre Unabhängigkeit von der Moderne proklamiert – von der einzigartigen Formensprache und der strengen Ideologie dieser Bewegung –, in der Praxis aber hat sie die alte Formensprache durch eine neue ersetzt, die sich in ihrer Symbolik von der alten unterscheidet, in ihrer Eigenheit aber dieser sehr ähnlich ist und die in ihrem Spektrum genauso begrenzt und in ihren Prinzipien genauso dogmatisch ist wie die alte. Die neue Bewegung verfügt nicht über die mannigfaltigen Symbole und die kulturelle Relevanz, die für unser Zeitalter angemessen wären. In dieser Hinsicht unterscheidet sie sich nicht von der vorangegangenen Bewegung. *Plus ça change...*

Die Postmoderne hat von der allgemeingültigen industriellen Formensprache der Moderne Abstand genommen. Wie wir in *Lernen von Las Vegas* feststellten, haben alle außer den Architekten gelernt, daß die Industrielle Revolution tot und deren fortdauernde Glorifizierung paradox ist. Wir hoben hervor, daß Le Corbusiers spätmoderner *béton-brut* in seiner Bedeutung antiindustriell gemeint war; angewandt durch seine Anhänger wurde er ausgesprochen heldenhaft und ebenso irrelevant wie die industrielle Formensprache, die er ersetzt hatte. Die Postmodernen jedoch haben, als sie die Modernen ablösten, die weitgehend irrelevante allgemeingültige Formensprache des heroischen Industrialismus durch eine andere weitgehend irrelevante allgemeingültige Formensprache ersetzt – nämlich der des emporkommenden Klassizismus mit – in seiner amerikanischen Variante – einem Schuß Art Deco und einem Hauch Ledoux. Indem sie die historische Symbolik durch eine der Moderne entsprechende ersetzten, schufen sie, nach Allgemeingültigkeit strebend, eine Art Neo-Klassizismus. Die Allgemeingültigkeit war den aristokratischen und republikanischen Herren des Neo-Klassizismus Ende des 18., Anfang des 19. Jahrhunderts und der im wesentlichen homogenen vorindustriellen Gesellschaftsstruktur, in der sie lebten, angemessen. Einer komplexen und pluralistischen postindustriellen Gesellschaft jedoch, wie die unsere es ist, kann sie nicht entsprechen. In diesem Zusammenhang waren die architektonischen Sprünge der 70er Jahre von Le Corbusier zu Ledoux, von Weiß- zu Pastelltönen nicht so groß wie sie scheinen mögen. Der Wechsel von den klaren und einfachen kubistischen Formen des Internationalen Stils zu den klaren und einfachen klassischen Formen des Neo-Klassizismus manifestiert die fortdauernde formalistische Vorliebe der Architekten für Vereinfachungen. Die weißen Formen jedoch sind heute mediterran gefärbt. Das gefällt den Bauherren, und die Projekte und Zeichnungen lassen sich besser verkaufen.

Mit einer Architektur, die formal schlicht und symbolisch schlüssig ist, kann man sich leicht identifizieren, sie ist leicht zu benennen, zu kopieren, zu erlernen, zu lehren, man kann leicht für sie werben, sie der Öffentlichkeit nahebringen, sie publizieren, sie zeichnen und sie ausstellen. Daß diese Architektur leicht zu benennen ist, wird durch die zahlreichen Bezeichnungen deutlich: Postmoderne, Rationalismus, Radikaler Eklektizismus, free-style Klassizismus, New Rules, etc. Aber täuscht nicht die Vielfalt ihrer Namen über ihren Mangel an Inhalt hinweg? Enthüllt nicht die Leichtigkeit und Schnelligkeit, mit der ihre Urheber sie benennen, ihre extreme Schlichtheit? Es gehört zu der Verantwortung der Historiker, Bewegungen und Stilrichtungen Namen zu geben. Wußte Bernini, daß er im Barock lebte? Architekten sollten ihre Arbeit

pure and simple Cubist forms of the International Style to the pure and simple Classical forms of Neo-classicism manifests architects' continuing formalist predilection for simplification. However, the white forms are now tinted in Mediterranean hues which pleases clients and makes projects and drawings more saleable.

Formal simplicity and symbolic consistency make architecture easy to identify, name, copy, learn, teach, promote, publicize, publish, draw and exhibit. That this architecture is easey to name is obvious by its proliferation of names: Post-modernism, Rationalism, Radical Eclecticism, Free-style Classicism, the New Rules, etc. But doesn't the variety of its names belie the paucity of its content? Doesn't the ease and speed with which its authors name it expose its over-simplicity? The naming of movements and styles is the historian's responsibility. Did Bernini know he was Baroque? Architects should describe their work, not name it. That Post-modernisme is easy to teach is obvious from its popularity among students and its acceptance in the architectural *academe* where archetypal simplification and easy universalities tend to be preferred to complexity and contradiction. That it is easy to promote is obvious because journalists love slogans. All this has obvious advantages and gives immediate satisfaction, but does it make for vigorous architecture that faces the complexities of reality?

Ledoux, in the context of the United States, is exotic as well as simplistic. I remember being startled at glimpsing out of the corner of my eye the Neo-classical city hall in the French Quarter of Montreal: it was a truly Neo-classical building. Having momentarily forgot I was in French Canada, I was subconsciously expecting a Greek Revival building typical of the United States —typical, indeed, of what I could have found immediately across the border in New York State. The differences between the pure, abstract, continental-Ledouxian version of Classicism and the more literal, sometimes naive, version of Doric that is Anglo-American, were, at his instant, subtle but telling.

If the symbolism of Post-modernism must be based on Classicism, why is it largely limited to Ledoux whose appropriateness on this continent beyond Quebec is questionable? The answer is because Ledoux is easy to take for former Modernists. He is one of the historical architects that Modern architects allowed themselves to admire and it is easy to move from liking him to doing him (douxing him and over-douxing him). He is also in vogue because of the influence within the Post-modern movement in this country of the Rationalist movement from Italy with its distinctly Latin version of Neo-Classicism. There are parallels here to the importation of the International Style to this continents in the '30s. Bauhaus architecture provided a similar strain of the exotic and irrelevant in the American context. Waxt an irony that many of those who now discredit the rigid impositions of the International Style now follow in its footsteps. *Encore plus ça change.* In advocating versions of Classical symbolism such as Grek Revival, Palladian, and Queen Anne that are varied and natural to our place and time —connected, that is, to our heritage— and employing them in our work, I am being realistic rather than chauvinistic, and rational more than Rationalist.

But why only Classical? In this paper I have discussed the rational for employing varieties of stules and employing applique and representation to achieve cultural relevance. In «A Definition of Architecture as Shelter with Decoration on It», I described a hypothetical building that sports a Serbo-Croatian front and a Mary Anne behind —its esthetic contradiction justified by conflicting demands of form and function and accommodated by its configuration as a decorated shed. The more traditional interdependence of form and function and the more literal and «serious» identification of form and symbol in Post-modernism, will not accommodate such functional contradictions. This tends to limit Post-modernism to a hierar-

beschreiben, nicht benennen. Daß die Postmoderne leicht zu unterrichten ist, wird offensichtlich angesichts der Popularität, der sie sich bei Studenten erfreut, und ihrer Anerkennung innerhalb der akademischen Architektur, wo man dazu neigt, archetypische Vereinfachungen und simple Allgemeingültigkeit der Komplexität und dem Widerspruch vorzuziehen. Daß sie leicht zu vermarkten ist, ist klar, weil Journalisten eine Vorliebe für Slogans haben. All dies hat augenscheinliche Vorteile und verschafft sofortige Befriedigung, aber wirkt es sich auch günstig aus auf eine ausdrucksstarke Architektur, die der Komplexität unserer Wirklichkeit standhält?

Ledoux ist, bezogen auf die Vereinigten Staaten, sowohl exotisch als auch simpel. Ich erinnere mich an mein Erstaunen, als ich aus dem Augenwinkel heraus das neo-klassizistische Rathaus im French Quarter von Montreal erblickte: Es war ein wahrhaft neo-klassizistisches Gebäude. Da ich einen Moment lang vergessen hatte, im französischsprachigen Teil Kanadas zu sein, hatte ich unbewußt ein Gebäude im Stil des griechischen Neo-Klassizismus erwartet, wie es für die Vereinigten Staaten typisch ist – in der Tat typisch für das, was ich gleich hinter der Grenze im Staat New York hätte antreffen können. Die Unterschiede zwischen der klaren, abstrakten, kontinentalen Ledoux-getreuen Version des Klassizismus und der wörtlichen, manchmal naiven Version des dorischen, das heißt anglo-amerikanischen, waren in diesem Augenblick subtil und aufschlußreich.

Wenn die Symbolik der Postmoderne auf dem Klassizismus basieren muß, warum wird sie dann weitgehend auf Ledoux beschränkt, dessen Eignung auf diesem Kontinent jenseits von Quebec fraglich ist? Die Antwort lautet: weil Ledoux für ehemalige Moderne leicht zu handhaben ist. Er ist einer der historischen Architekten, den Architekten der Moderne zu bewundern sich gestatten, und schnell geht man vom ihn mögen zum ihn bauen über (zum ihn douxen und über-douxen!). Auch wegen dem Einfluß, den der Rationalismus aus Italien mit seiner ausgeprägten römischen Spielart des Neo-Klassizismus auf die Postmoderne in diesem Land ausübt, ist er en vogue. Hier gibt es Parallelen zum Import des Internationalen Stils auf diesen Kontinent während der 30er Jahre. Die Bauhaus-Architektur weist in ihrer amerikanischen Variante einen ähnlichen Hang zum Exotischen und Irrelevanten auf. Welch eine Ironie, daß viele von denen, die nun die strengen Zwänge des Internationalen Stils in Mißkredit bringen, gleichzeitig in seine Fußstapfen treten. *Encore plus ça change.* Indem ich Formen der klassischen Symbolik wie des griechischen Neo-Klassizismus, des Palladianismus und der Queen-Anne-Architektur befürworte, die reichhaltig und naturgemäß sind für unseren Raum und unsere Zeit – in einem Zusammenhang stehen, mit unserem Erbe nämlich – und diese in unserer Arbeit anwende, bin ich eher realistisch als chauvinistisch, eher rational als rationalistisch.

Aber warum nur aus der Klassik? In diesem Buch habe ich Gründe für die Anwendung unterschiedlichster Stilarten, Applikationen und Darstellungen aufgeführt, um kulturelle Relevanz zu erzielen. In »Architektur als dekorierte Hülle« beschrieb ich ein hypothetisches Gebäude, das eine serbokroatische Front und eine Rückfront im Schema »F« hat – seine ästhetische Widersprüchlichkeit wurde gerechtfertigt durch miteinander im Konflikt stehende Ansprüche an Form und Funktion, und durch ihre Zusammenstellung als dekorierter Schuppen wurde derselben Rechnung getragen. Die eher traditionelle gegenseitige Abhängigkeit von Form und Funktion und die eher wörtliche und »ernsthafte« Gleichstellung von Form und Symbol in der Postmoderne kann solchen funktionalen Widersprüchen nicht Rechnung tragen. Deshalb wird man die Postmoderne auf eine Reihe traditioneller Gebäudetypen, Gebäude für Institutionen und städtische Gebäude beschränken – die Gebäudetypen, die mit dem Klassizismus assoziiert werden können – obwohl, und dies ist für Amerikaner befremdend, neo-klassizistische Arbeiterhäuser in Norditalien sich gut vertragen mit kommunistischen Bürgermeistern.

Aber umfaßt die Architektur nicht auch gewöhnliche Häuser? Ich habe den Entwurf für einen Ausstellungsraum in äußerst getreuem klassizistischen Stil

chy of traditional building types and to institutional and civic buildings —the range of building types associated with Classicism— although, strangely to Americans, Neo-classical workers' housing seems to sit weel with Communist mayors in Northern Italy.

But doesn't architecture encompass ordinary buildngs too? I've seen a design for a catalog showroom in a highly literal Classical style. As a Post-modern building it was, to me, distinctly uncomfortable; as a decorated shed sporting Classical representation, it would have come off. Another recent design for a quarter in Paris is an exquisite collage of axes *a la* Le Notre (*au Notre?*). Hausmannian boulevards intersect delightful streets whose widths perfectly balance the heights of Classical façades, whose sky is punctuated by high-diving by-wing planes seemingly piloted by World War I aces. The pedestrian density of this urban fabric would appeal to any antiquarian who strolls the streets of the 18th century quarters of Paris or parts of Munich or Leningrad, but what about the reality of cars on the ground (over drawings of Messerschmidts in the air) in the late 20th century, and the right of our cities to be civic and residential *and* commercial in their function, and of their symbolism to be nostalgic *and* real?

A plea for pattern all over

In this critique of Post-modernism I have emphasized historicism in architecture because this is the chief feature of that movement, and I have advocated an explicitly symbolic and representational historicism that is conveyed through applique. To put it another way, I have been concerned with ornament whose content is historical. But there is another type of ornament that has been acknowledged but little employed by Post-modernists perhaps because of their lingering Modernist prediliction for simplicity and the predominating influence of Italian Rationalism. This ornament consists of over-all pattern. It is an ornamental direction of enormous range and potential. Pattern-ornament can be abstract, as in the decorative tile or brick surfaces of Moslem architecture —among the supremely beautiful and complex creations in the history of art. It can be representational, as in figured Byzantine mosaics or in the pretty floral wallpapers of Victorian interiors. It can be symbolically architectural, as in the façades of those Italian Romanesque churches (5) whose rows of *bas-relief* arcades crash into portal, rose window, or moulding, seeming discordant and lyrical at once.

Our additions to the Oberlin Art Museum, I.S.I. office building, and Best Products Showroom are decorated sheds where geometric and floral patterns are appliqued using masonry and porcelainized panels. In the Best showroom loft, big flowers, bold *and pretty,* camouflage the inevitable banality of the architectural form and read as a sign across a vast parking lot and speedy highway. Ornament that is pattern-all-over is currently the subject of painters of the Patterns and Decoration Movement in New York. These painters have acknowledged an inevitable reaction against the Minimalism of late Modern esthetics. As with the American Pop Art and Photorealist movements, the painters are ahead of the architects in their esthetic sensibility. Architects too, I think, will have to recognize the impracticality of expressionist heroics, on one hand, and of Minimalist indulgence on the other, and acknowledge the potential for richness in the decorated shed —and eventually in the decorated car, the decorated anything all over our environment.

In this argument I have cast Modern architecture in a bad role, but I want to qualify my attitude toward the Modern movement and distinguish it from that of many of the Post-modernists. I have never intended totally to reject Modern architecture in words or work, because I do, and I think our architecture should, in many important ways, evolve out of it, not revolt from it. Its masterpieces hold their own with those of any age. For-

gesehen. Als postmodernes Gebäude wirkte es auf mich ausgesprochen ungemütlich, als dekorierter Schuppen, Klassizismus darstellend, hätte ich es verkraftet. Ein anderer kürzlicher Entwurf für ein Viertel in Paris ist eine exquisite Collage von Achsen à la Le Notre. Boulevards im Stil Hausmanns schneiden auf wunderbare Weise Straßen, deren Breite genau abgestimmt ist auf die Höhen der klassizistischen Fassaden; der Himmel ist durchsetzt mit tieffliegenden Doppeldeckern, die anscheinend von Starpiloten des 1. Weltkriegs gesteuert werden. Die Fußgängerdichte dieser Stadtstruktur würde jedem Antiquitätenhändler zusagen, der durch die Straßen des 18. Jahrhunderts schlenderte, so es in Paris oder in Teilen Münchens oder Leningrads, aber was ist mit der Realität der Autos auf der Erde Ende des 20. Jahrhunderts (die so viel präsenter ist als die Darstellungen der Messerschmidts in der Luft), und dem Recht unserer Städte, bürgerlich und wohnlich *und* kommerziell in ihrer Funktion zu sein sowie dem Recht ihrer Symbolik, nostalgisch *und* wirklich zu sein?

Plädoyer für ein Muster total

In dieser Kritik der Postmoderne betonte ich besonders den Historismus in der Architektur als dem Hauptmerkmal dieser Bewegung, und ich machte mich stark für einen explizit symbolischen und repräsentativen Historismus, der durch Applikationen vermittelt wird. Anders ausgedrückt, ich sprach über Ornamente, deren Inhalt historisch ist. Es gibt aber noch eine Art von Ornamenten, die von Anhängern der Postmoderne zwar anerkannt, aber wenig verwendet werden, vielleicht wegen ihrer ausgedehnten modernistischen Vorliebe für Schlichtheit und dem vorherrschenden Einfluß des italienischen Rationalismus. Dieses Ornament besteht aus alles überlagernden Mustern. Diese dekorative Richtung verfügt über eine enorme Bandbreite und ebensolche Möglichkeiten. Das Ornament als Muster kann abstrakt sein, wie in den dekorativen Fliesen- oder Ziegeloberflächen der moslemischen Architektur – sie gehören zu den schönsten und reichsten Schöpfungen der Kunstgeschichte. Es kann aber auch repräsentativ sein, wie im Fall der byzantinischen figurativen Mosaike oder der schönen Blumentapeten der viktorianischen Innenräume. Es kann Architektur symbolisieren, wie auf den Fassaden der italienischen romanischen Kirchen (5), deren Reihen von *bas-relief* Arkaden in das Portal, die Fensterrose oder das Gesims laufen und die disharmonisch und lyrisch zugleich wirken.

Unsere Anbauten an das Oberlin Art Museum, dem I.S.I. Bürogebäude und dem Best Products Showroom sind dekorierte Schuppen, bei denen wir geometrische und florale Muster aufbrachten mittels Mauerwerk und Paneelen mit porzellan-emaillierten Oberflächen. Der obere Teil des Best Showroom wurde von uns mit großen, ausdrucksvollen *und schönen* Blumen überzogen, die so die unvermeidbare Banalität der architektonischen Form tarnen und gleichzeitig als Zeichen quer über den riesigen Parkplatz und von der schnell befahrenen Landstraße aus erkennbar sind. Das Ornament als alles-überlagerndes Muster ist momentan Hauptthema der Maler des Pattern and Decoration Movement in New York. Diese Maler haben die unvermeidliche Reaktion gegen den Minimalismus der Ästhetik der späten Moderne verarbeitet. Genau wie bei der Pop Art und bei den Photorealisten in Amerika sind die Maler mit ihrer ästhetischen Sensibilität den Architekten voraus. Ich glaube, daß auch die Architekten erkennen müssen, daß expressionistische Heldentaten einerseits und die Erfordernisse des Minimalismus andererseits nicht vereinbar sind und das reiche Potential, das im dekorierten Schuppen liegt, anerkennen müssen – und schließlich beim dekorierten Auto und allem Dekorierten in unserer gesamten Umwelt.

In diesem Sinne habe ich die Architektur der Moderne in ein schlechtes Licht gerückt, möchte aber meine Einstellung ihr gegenüber näher erläutern und sie von der vieler Anhänger der Postmoderne unterscheiden. Es war nie meine Absicht, die Architektur der Moderne völlig abzulehnen, weder durch Worte noch durch Taten, denn ich entwickle, genau wie es die Architekten überhaupt tun sollten, meine Architektur aus ihr heraus und nicht gegen sie.

getting the Rococo perhaps, the Modern was the first style since the Gothic to be based on an original symbolism (acknowledging its immediate derivation from the industrial vernacular of its time). Today we focus on its excesses and weaknesses at the end, to the exclusion of its successes and glory at the beginning. This makes us want to be revolutionary rather than evolutionary, anti-Modern rather than truly Post-modern.

One of the flaws of the Modern movement was its revolutionary zeal, its progressive rejection of the past. It is ironic that many critics of the rigidity and exclusiveness of Modernism who now fervently proclaim their liberation from its bondage display an equal, if opposite, revolutionary zeal; some of today's most intolerant Post-modern architects were «Whites» last year. It is too easy to hate our fathers in attempting to transcend them. In so doing we find refuge once again from a complex and contradictory world in simple formulas for our work and simple dogmas for our philosophy. Denise Scott Brown wrote in our preface to *Learning from Las Vegas:* «Since we have criticized Modern architecture, it is proper here to state our intense admiration of its early period when its founders, sensitive to their own times, proclaimed the right revolution. Our argument lies mainly with the irrelevant and distorted prolongation of that old revolution today». And now with that old revolution in a new guise.

A postscript on my mother's house

Although I am critical of much of the Classicism I see in Post-modern architecture, and because I am frequently dismissed as a Pop architect, I would like to make it plain that I consider myself an architect who adheres to the Classical tradition of Western architecture. I claim that my approach and the substance of my work are Classical, and have been from the beginning of my career. My mother's house in Chestnut Hill, Philadelphia (6,7) the second building of my design to be built, is an explicitly Classical building in the substance of its plan and form and in the ornament of its elevations. This was unusual in 1964, the year of its completion.

But the house, though Classical, is not pure. Within the Classical esthetic it conforms to a Mannerist tradition which admits contradiction within the ideal order and thereby enhances the ideal quality of that order through contrast with it. To perceive the ideal you must acknowledge the real. Contradiction in Classical architecture manifest in distortion and exception occurs in the work of Palladio and many others who are my guides.

Some Classical and contradictory aspects of my mother's house are: (8,9,13) the plan and the front and back elevations are symmetrical about a central axis, but, within the consistent perimeter of the plan the extremities vary to accommodate exceptions in plan, and within the consistent profile of the elevations, the extremities vary to conform to exceptions within; the configuration of windows is asymmetrical, if balanced, for the same reason. The central core of the house is a solid, not the void typical of a Palladian plan. The solid core consists of a fireplace, chimney, and stair, like that of a New England house of the 17th century. The central entrance reads on the front elevation as a void, rather big in scale like that of a porticoed Palladian villa, but it is contradicted by the blank set-back wall of the solid core which is itself distorted in plan to accommodate circulation around it. Symmetry in plan is therefore modified at the extremities via exceptions, and nearer the center via distortions.

The front and back elevations are Classically symmetrical with strong centralities. The front elevations is a Classical pediment (12); this façade-as-pediment I derived from the pavilion at the rear of Palladio's Villa Maser. A gable end as a front elevation was unusual in 1964. This gable is also a split pediment to reveal the central chimney block behind, to enhance the Mannerist effect of spatial layering, and to make of the façade thereby a king of disengaged sign. The façade as disengaged pediment

Ihre Meisterwerke können sich behaupten wie die jedes anderen Zeitalters. Wenn man das Rokoko vielleicht außer acht läßt, dann war die Moderne seit der Gotik die erste Stilrichtung, die auf einer ihr eigenen Symbolik beruht (indem man ihre unmittelbare Ableitung von der industriellen Formensprache ihrer Zeit anerkennt). Heute konzentrieren wir uns auf ihre am Ende auftretenden Ausschweifungen und Schwächen und schließen ihre anfänglichen Erfolge und ihren Ruhm aus. Dies veranlaßt uns, lieber revolutionär als evolutionär sein zu wollen, lieber anti-modern als wirklich post-modern.

Einer der Mängel der Moderne war ihr revolutionärer Eifer, ihre zunehmende Ablehnung des Vergangenen. Es ist schon paradox, daß viele Kritiker der Strenge und Ausschließlichkeit der Moderne, die jetzt inbrünstig die Befreiung von ihrer Unterjochung proklamieren, den gleichen, wenn auch entgegengesetzten, revolutionären Eifer an den Tag legen; so mancher der heutigen äußerst intoleranten Architekten der Postmoderne war letztes Jahr noch Anhänger der »Whites«. Es ist zu einfach, dem Haß auf unsere Väter Ausdruck zu geben dadurch, daß wir versuchen, sie zu übertreffen. Wenn wir so handeln, finden wir wieder einmal Zuflucht vor einer komplexen und widersprüchlichen Welt in einfachen Formeln für unsere Arbeit und in einfachen Dogmen für unsere Philosophie. Denise Scott Brown schrieb in unserem Vorwort zu *Lernen von Las Vegas:* »Da wir die Architektur der Moderne kritisiert haben, ist es angebracht, hier unsere tiefe Bewunderung für ihre frühe Phase zum Ausdruck zu bringen, als ihre Begründer, empfänglich für die Zeichen ihrer Zeit, die richtige Revolution proklamierten. Unsere Kritik bezieht sich hauptsächlich auf die irrelevante und verzerrte Fortsetzung dieser alten Revolution heute.« Und heute haben wir diese alte Revolution in einer neuen Gestalt.

Ein Postskriptum zum Haus meiner Mutter

Obwohl ich vielen Aspekten des Klassizismus, die ich in der Architektur der Postmoderne sehe, kritisch gegenüberstehe und weil ich häufig als Pop-Architekt abgetan werde, möchte ich hier einmal in aller Deutlichkeit klarstellen, daß ich mich selbst als einen Architekten betrachte, der an der klassischen Tradition der westlichen Architektur festhält. Ich behaupte, daß meine Versuche und der Kern meiner Arbeit in der klassischen Tradition liegen und daß dies seit Beginn meiner Laufbahn so ist. Das Haus meiner Mutter in Chestnut Hill, Philadelphia (6, 7), das zweite von mir entworfene Gebäude, das gebaut wurde, ist durch seinen Grundriß, seine Form und durch die Ornamente seiner Fassaden ein ausgesprochen klassisches Gebäude. 1964, dem Jahr seiner Fertigstellung, war es ungewöhnlich.

Obwohl das Haus klassisch ist, ist es dennoch nicht Klassik in ihrer reinsten Form. Innerhalb der klassischen Ästhetik entspricht es einer manieristischen Tradition, die Widersprüche innerhalb der idealen Ordnung zuläßt und dabei die ideale Qualität dieser Ordnung verbessert, indem sie nämlich einen Kontrast zu ihr bildet. Um die ideale Form zu erreichen, muß man die Realität anerkennen. Im Werk Palladios und vieler anderer, die ich zu meinen Vorbildern zähle, kommen Widersprüche innerhalb der klassischen Architektur vor, in Form von Verzerrungen und Abweichungen.

Einige klassische und widersprüchliche Aspekte im Haus meiner Mutter sind: (8, 9, 13) Der Grundriß und die Vorder- und Rückfassade sind symmetrisch zu einer Mittelachse angeordnet, aber innerhalb der durchgehenden Außenbegrenzung des Grundrisses ist es möglich, Abweichungen an den äußeren Enden im Plan Rechnung zu tragen, und trotz einer durchgängigen Fassade variieren die äußeren Begrenzungen, um Abweichungen dahinter aufzunehmen; aus dem selben Grund sind die Fenster asymmetrisch, wenn auch ausgewogen, angeordnet. Die Mitte des Hauses ist massiv, nicht offen, wie es für einen Grundriß Palladios typisch ist. Der massive Kern birgt Feuerstelle, Kamin und Treppe, so wie es im 17. Jahrhundert in den Häusern Neuenglands gemacht wurde. Die Vorderfront ist durch den zentralen Eingang aufgebrochen, der groß dimensioniert ist wie der Portikus einer palladianischen Villa. Dem wird aber die freistehende zurückgesetzte Wand des massiven or abstracted sign (10) is also reinforced by the parapets of the front and back walls which make them seem independent of the roof and siedes of the house. In the rear elevation the central element is the big arched window less than a semi-circle in shape. As in Neo-classical façades, it promotes big scale and grand unity in a small pavilion.

Perhaps the most unusual feature of these elevations for 1964 was their applied decoration with its Classical character (11). There is a dado on the front and back elevations. It consists of a wood moulding, placed a little high in terms of Classical precedent to enhance the scale of a small building. A shallow arch composed of the same moulding, is applied above the entrance opening. The arch is juxtaposed on the concrete lintel that sits flush with the stucco wall. Arch and lintel together further enhance the scale of the already relatively big central opening. This use of ornamental redundancy and Classical association completes the Classical composition of the whole. The abstract linear quality of the Classical ornament applied to the smooth plaster walls, together with the disengagement of the walls at the parapets, makes the façades look almost like drawings and enhances their quality as representations of Classical architecture.

There are important elements of this design which are not Classical: for example, the industrial sash and the strip window of the kitchen. But these act as counterpoint; they form part of the Classical-Mannerist element of contradiction within the whole and they establish this architecture as evolving Modern as well as reviving Classical. I did not explain this house as explicitly Classical in *Complexity and Contradiction in Architecture* because in the 1960s I was more interested in describing its Mannerist than its Classical qualities. I did, however, make analogies with historical Classical architecture in my description of the building, and this has since become a Post-modernist literary device.

The Classicism that is essential to my mother's house is typical of most of the buildings I have designed. These buildings are Castle Howard[2]-as-built, with the ultimate asymmetry of its north front rather than Castle Howard-as-designed, with its unbroken symmetry, but they are Castle Howard nonetheless.

In the end I am speaking of a historicist symbolism that seeks the essence of a style —or a place, or a tradition. I hope that my mother's house achieves an essence of Classicism in its conext; for achieving essence is our ultimate aim in using symbolism in architecture— but that is the subject of another paper.

Some have said my mother's house looks like a child's drawing of a house (14) —representing the fundamental elements of shelter— gable roof, chimney, door, and windows. I like to think this is so, that it achieves another essence, that of the genre that is house and is elemental.

Notes

1. Denise Scott Brown, «A Worm's Eye View of Recent Architectural History», in *Essays on the Current State of Architecture,* Peter Eisenman, ed. Institute for Architecture and Urban Studies and Rizzoli International Inc., New York; 1982.

2. Castle Howard was designed by Sir John Vanbrugh and Nicholas Hawksmoor in 1702-32 and is in Yorkshire, England.

Kerns gegenübergesetzt, die in ihrem Grundriß gekrümmt ist, um Platz zu machen für die Erschließung. Die Symmetrie innerhalb des Grundrisses ist an ihren äußersten Punkten durch Ausnahmen und der Mitte zu durch Verzerrungen modifiziert.

Die Vorder- und Rückfassaden sind klassisch symmetrisch und streng zentriert. Die Vorderfront stellt einen klassischen Ziergiebel dar (12); diese Fassade als Ziergiebel ist abgeleitet vom Pavillon auf der Rückseite der von Palladio entworfenen Villa Maser. Die Vorderfront als Giebel auszubilden war 1964 ungewöhnlich. Dieser Giebel ist auch ein aufgebrochener Ziergiebel, um den dahinter befindlichen zentralen Kamin erkennbar zu machen, die manieristische Wirkung der räumlichen Schichtung zu betonen und so die Fassade als ein ausdrucksstarkes losgelöstes Zeichen wirken zu lassen. Die Wirkung der Fassade als selbständiger Ziergiebel oder abstrahiertes Zeichen (10) wird noch verstärkt durch die oberen Abschlüsse der vorderen und rückwärtigen Wandscheiben, die diese losgelöst von Dach und Seitenwänden erscheinen lassen. Das zentrale Element in der rückwärtigen Wand ist ein großes gebogenes Fenster, seiner Form nach etwas kleiner als ein Halbkreis. Wie in neoklassizistischen Fassaden bewirkt es Großzügigkeit und Geschlossenheit in einem kleinen Pavillon.

Das für 1964 wohl ungewöhnlichste Element dieser Fassaden war die verwendete Verzierung im klassischen Stil (11). An der Vorder- und Rückseite ist jeweils ein Sockel angebracht. Er besteht aus einer Holzzierleiste, die, gemessen an ihrem klassischen Vorbild, etwas hoch angebracht ist, um das kleine Haus größer wirken zu lassen. Ein leicht geschwungener Bogen aus derselben Zierleiste ist über dem Eingang angebracht. Der Bogen sitzt auf dem Betonsturz, der mit der Putzwand bündig abschließt. Bogen und Sturz zusammen lassen wiederum die Ausmaße der relativ großen zentralen Öffnung noch größer erscheinen. Die großzügige Verwendung von Dekorationen und klassischen Anspielungen vervollständigt die klassische Komposition des Ganzen. Die abstrakte lineare Eigenschaft der auf die glatten Putzwände aufgebrachten klassischen Dekoration und die Tatsache, daß die Wände an ihren oberen Begrenzungen losgelöst wirken, bewirkt, daß die Fassaden fast wie gezeichnet aussehen und unterstreicht ihre Eigenschaft als Abbild klassischer Architektur.

In diesem Entwurf gibt es wichtige Elemente, die nicht klassisch sind, wie zum Beispiel das Industriefenster und das Fensterband in der Küche. Diese wirken aber als Kontrapunkt; sie bilden einen Teil des klassisch-manieristischen Elements des Widerspruchs innerhalb des Ganzen und machen deutlich, daß diese Architektur sowohl eine sich entwickelnde moderne als auch eine sich wiederbelebende klassische ist. In *Komplexität und Widerspruch in der Architektur* habe ich dieses Haus nicht als ausgesprochen klassisch bezeichnet, denn in den 60er Jahren lag mir mehr daran, eher seine manieristischen als seine klassischen Eigenschaften zu beschreiben. In meiner Beschreibung des Gebäudes stellte ich jedoch Analogien zur historischen klassischen Architektur auf, und das ist seitdem zu einem literarischen Kunstgriff der Postmoderne geworden.

Der Klassizismus beim Haus meiner Mutter ist typisch für die meisten Gebäude, die ich gezeichnet habe. Sie sind eher im Stil Castle Howard² wie es gebaut wurde, mit der asymmetrischen Nordfassade, als im Stil von Castle Howard wie es entworfen wurde.

Schließlich spreche ich noch über eine historisierende Symbolik, die das Wesen eines Stils, eines Orts oder einer Tradition anstrebt. Ich hoffe, das Haus meiner Mutter wird das Wesen des Klassizismus erreichen, ist es doch unser höchstes Ziel, Tiefe zu erreichen, wenn wir Symbole in der Architektur verwenden – aber das ist Thema eines anderen Buches.

Manche Leute behaupten, das Haus meiner Mutter sehe aus wie die Kinderzeichnung eines Hauses (14) – mit den wesentlichen Elementen einer Hülle – Giebeldach, Kamin, Tür und Fenster. Mir gefällt, daß man so darüber denkt, daß das Haus einen anderen Inhalt bekommt, nämlich den, ein Haus zu sein und elementaren Charakter zu haben.

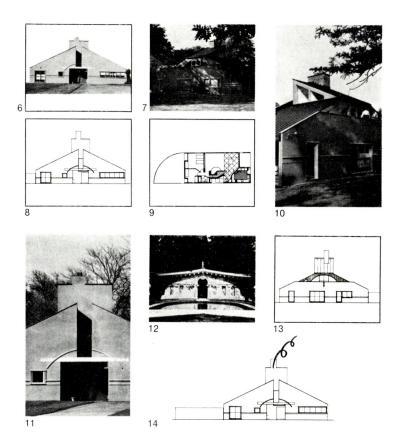

6. Haus Vanna Venturi, Philadelphia. Foto: Rollin La France
7. Ansicht von hingen. Foto: George Pohl
8. Ansicht von vorne
9. Grundriß Erdgeschoß
10. Ansicht von hinten mit Balkon. Foto: George Pohl
11. Detail der Vorderansicht. Foto: Rollin La France
12. Pavillion, Villa Barbaro, Maser
13. Ansicht von hinten
14. Ansicht von vorne mit *graffiti*

6. Vanna Venturi House, Philadelphia; Rollin La France photo
7. Rear view; George Pohl photo
8. Front elevation
9. First floor plan
10. Rear view showing parapets; George Pohl photo
11. Detail of front elevation; Rollin La France photo
12. Rear pavilion, Villa Barbaro at Maser
13. Rear elevation
14. Front elevation with graffiti

Anmerkungen

1 Denise Scott Brown: »Die jüngste Architekturgeschichte aus der Froschperspektive«, in: *Essays on the current State of Architecture,* Peter Eisenman, Hrsg., Institute for Architecture and Urban Studies and Rizzoli International Inc., New York; 1982.
2 Castle Howard wurde 1702–32 von Sir John Vanbrugh und Nicholas Hawksmoor entworfen und steht in Yorkshire, England.

Haus am Meer. Projekt, 1959
Robert Venturi

Dieses Wochenendhaus in den Dünen des Strandes ist zum Meer hin ausgerichtet. Es verfügt nur über die einfachsten Wohneinrichtungen, da die Bewohner wohl den größten Teil des Tages am Strand verbringen. Auf der dem Meer zugewandten Seite befindet sich eine kleine Terrasse und ein offener Aussichtsturm auf dem Dach, erreichbar über eine Leiter und eine neben dem Kamin gelegene Falltür.

Das Haus hat eigentlich nur zwei Ansichten: die Vorderfront, die dem Meer zugewandt ist, und die rückwärtige Fassade mit dem Eingang. Es hat sozusagen keine Seiten, und die Vorderfront unterscheidet sich von der rückwärtigen, um ihre Ausrichtung zum Meer hin zu unterstreichen. Vom offenen Kamin aus, der in der Mitte des hinteren Teils gelegen ist, laufen die diagonalen Wände zunächst symmetrisch und bilden so die Innenräume. Wegen dieser komplexen Anordnung in der Fassade und im Grundriß ist das Dach als Giebelwalm-

House at the Sea. Project, 1959
Robert Venturi

This weekend cottage, set among dunes on a beach, is to face to view of the ocean. It contains the simplest living accommodations, since the inhabitants are expected to spend most of the day on the beach. There is a small terrace on the ocean front and an open belvedere on the roof accessible by ladder and trap near the chimney.

Expressively, the house has only two elevations: the front, oriented toward the sea, and the back for entering. It has no sides, so to speak; and the front is different from the back to express its directional inflection toward the ocean view. The fireplace-chimney at the rear center is a focus for the diagonal walls, which radiate, at first symmetrically, to form the inner spaces. Because of these complex configurations in elevation and plan, the roof is hipped and gabled at the same time, and its original symmetrical form is distorted ar the extremities of the building by varying interior demands, and by exterior for-

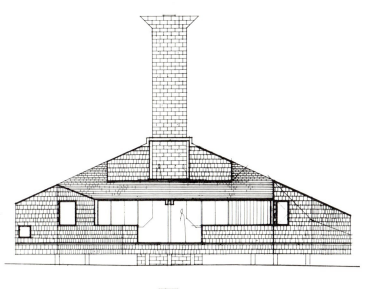

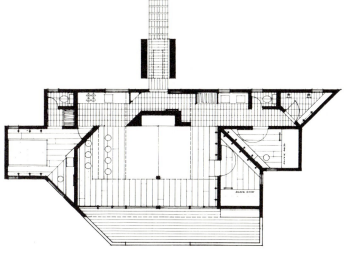

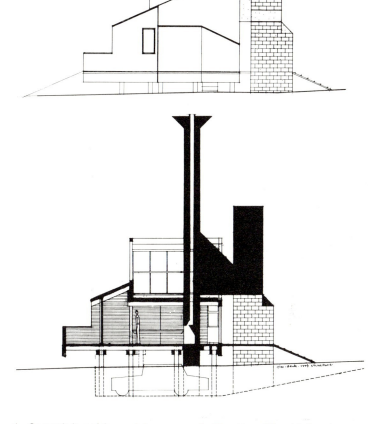

1. Gesamtansicht des Modells	4. Seitliche Fassade
2. Seitenansicht des Modells	5. Grundriß
3. Rückwärtige Fassade	6. Querschnitt

1. General view of the model	4. Elevation of the side façade
2. Side view of the model	5. Plan
3. Elevation of the rear façade	6. Crosswise section

dach ausgebildet, und seine ursprünglich symmetrische Form ist an den äußeren Enden des Gebäudes verfremdet, um den Erfordernissen des Innenraums sowie der äußeren Ausrichtung Rechnung zu tragen. Am spitzen Ende dominiert der Anspruch auf eine ausdrucksstarke äußere Form des Hauses »ohne Seiten«, das so konzipiert wurde, über die sekundären räumlichen Erfordernisse einer Dusche im Innenraum.

ces of orientation and view. At the pointed end, the exterior spatial-expressive demands of a house «without sides», directed toward the view, dominate the secondary spatial needs of a shower inside.

Haus Pearson. Projekt. Philadelphia, Pennsylvania, 1959
Robert Venturi

In diesem Entwurf liegen Elemente in Elementen und hinter Elementen. Zugrunde lag die Idee kontrastierender räumlicher Schichten zwischen Innen- und Außenraum, im Grundriß durch eine Reihe parallel verlaufender Wände und im Schnitt durch eine offene innere Deckenhaube, die durch diagonal verlaufende Rahmen gestützt wird; die Idee, kontrapunktisch, rhythmisch gegenübergestellter Stützenöffnungen in der Vorhalle, unterer und oberer Fenster und der Oberlichte über der inneren Deckenkuppel, und schließlich die Idee einer Reihe nebeneinanderliegender gleichförmiger Räume ohne Zweckbestimmung, unterbrochen von dienenden Räumen mit spezifischer Form und Funktion.

Pearson House. Project. Philadelphia, Pennsylvania, 1959
Robert Venturi

This project for a house involves things in things and things behind things. It exploits the idea of contrasting spatial layers between the inside and the outside in the series of parallel walls in plan and in the open inner domes supported on diagonal frames in section; the idea of contrapuntal, rhythmic juxtaposition in the relation of the pier openings of the porch, and of the lower and upper windows and of the cupolas above the inner domes; and the idea of a series of spaces in suite which are general in shape and unspecific in function, separated by servant spaces specific in shape and function.

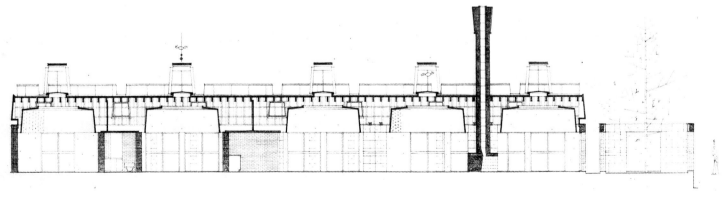

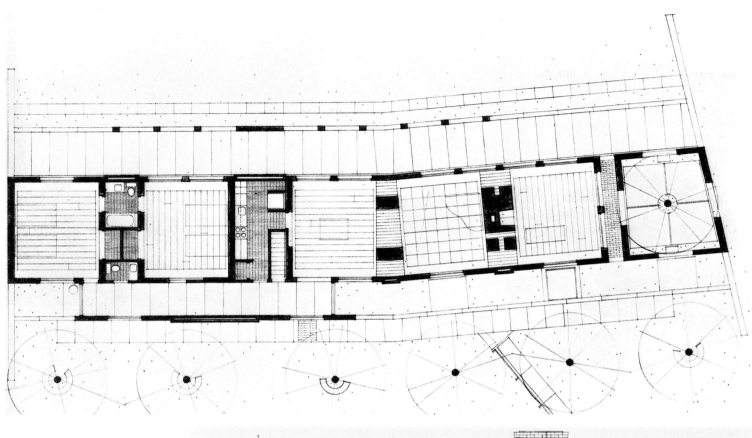
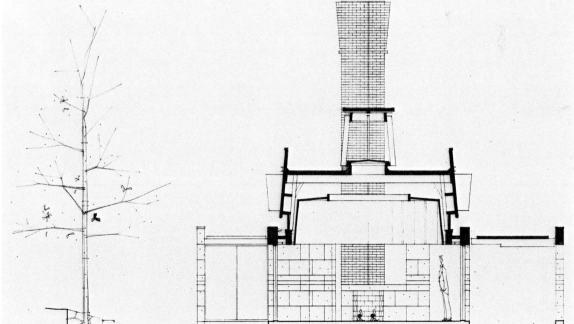

1. Gesamtansicht des Modells
2. Längsschnitt
3. Grundriß
4. Querschnitt

1. General view of the model
2. Lengthwise section
3. Plan
4. Crosswise section

Umgestaltung des Duke House, Institute of Fine Arts, New York University, New York City, 1959
Robert Venturi
Fotos: Leni Iselin

Diese Villa an der oberen Fifth Avenue war eine Schenkung an das Institute of Fine Arts, um als Graduate School für Kunstgeschichte genutzt zu werden. 1912 wurde sie von Horace Trumbauer entworfen. Grundgedanke war, innen so wenig wie möglich zu verändern und durch ein kontrastierendes Nebeneinander eine Harmonie von alt und neu zu erreichen; die Verbindung zwischen alten und neuen Elementen zu unterstreichen, eher durch Hinzufügen neuer als durch Veränderung bestehender innerer Elemente eine Veränderung zu schaffen, die neuen Bauteile eher als Möblierung denn als Architektur zu verstehen und Möbel und Ausstattungsgegenstände zu benutzen, die alltäglich und allgemein gebräuchlich sind, durch ihre ungewöhnliche Anwendung jedoch auffallen.

Duke House Renovation, Institute of Fine Arts, New York University, New York City, 1959.
Robert Venturi
Photography: Leni Iselin

This mansion on upper Fifth Avenue was donated to the Institute of Fine Arts for use as a graduate school of the History of Art. It was designed by Horace Trumbauer in 1912. The approach was to touch the inside as little as possible and to create harmony between the old and the new through contrasting juxtapositions; to separate the joint between the old and the new layers, to create change by adding to rather than modifying existing interior elements, to consider the new elements furniture rather than architecture and to use furniture and equipment which is commonplace and standard but enhanced by its uncommon setting.

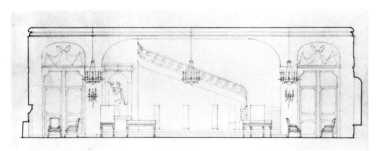

1. Schnitt durch die Halle
2. Perspektivische Ansicht der Halle
3. Perspektivische Ansicht des Flurs mit der Wendeltreppe am Ende
4. Detail der Bücherregalbefestigung
5. Detail des Handlaufs
6. Innenraumansicht

1. Section through the hall
2. Perspective of the hall
3. Perspective of a corridor with the spiral staircase at the end
4. Detail of insertion of the bookcases
5. Detail of the stair's handrail
6. Interior view

Verwaltungszentrale der Krankenschwesternvereinigung North Pennsylvania, Ambler, Pennsylvania, 1962
Robert Venturi
Mitarbeiter: Stanford Anderson
Fotos: George Phol

Wirtschaftliche Gründe schrieben ein kleines, konventionelles Gebäude vor. Die Umgebung legte einen kühnen Entwurf und eine einfache Form nahe, um einen Ausgleich zu den umliegenden großen Gebäuden zu schaffen. Das Programm verlangte eine komplexe Innenraumaufteilung, die jedoch unterschiedliche Räume und spezielle Lagermöglichkeiten beinhalten mußte. Ebenerdige Stellplätze für fünf Autos der Angestellten auf dem steil ansteigenden Gelände machten einen von einer Stützmauer begrenzten Parkhof an der Vorderseite notwendig. Da ein Eingang mit möglichst wenig Außenstufen verlangt wurde, mußte das Gebäude direkt an der Straße liegen.

Das entstandene Gebäude ist ein verzerrter Kubus, einfach und komplex zugleich. Da sie nebeneinander liegen und ähnlich geformt sind, bilden Hof und Gebäude eine Zweiheit. Die zum Hof hin spitz auslaufende Ecke des Gebäudes löst die Dualität zwar einerseits auf, andererseits jedoch verstärkt die Verzerrung des kubischen Gebäudes diese Dualität wieder, indem sie sich mit der gebogenen Mauer an der gegenüberliegenden Seite des Parkplatzes ergänzt, den Hof symmetrischer erscheinen läßt und ihn so von dem Gebäude

Headquarters Building of the North Pennsylvania Nurse Association, Ambler, Pennsylvania, 1962
Robert Venturi
Collaborator: Stanford Anderson
Photography: George Pohl

Economy dictated a small building with conventional construction. The setting suggested a bold scale and a simple form to compensate for the large buildings around. The program dictated a complex inside, however, with varieties of spaces and special storage accommodations. Level parking for five staff cars on the steeply sloping site necessitated a retaining-walled auto court up front. And a pedestrian entrance with a minimum of outside steps similarly dictated a building immediately on the street.

The resultant building is a distorted box both simple and complex. Because they are adjacent and similar in area, the court and the building set up a duality. The prow of the building acts as an inflection toward the court to resolve the duality, yet this distortion of the boxlike building simultaneously enforces the duality by complementing the curved wall at the opposite side of the parking court and by making the court more symmetrical and, therefore, independent of the building. The building at this point is more sculptural than architectural. Outside spatial forces dominate the interior forces, and it is designed from the outside in. The «awkward» interior created here is a subordinate space —merely the dentist's dark room.

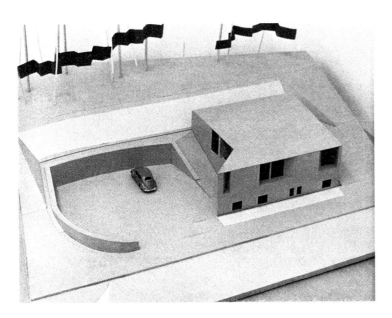
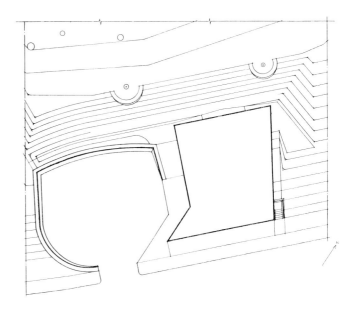

abhebt. So gesehen wirkt das Gebäude eher wie eine Skulptur denn als Architektur. Die äußeren räumlichen Zwänge beherrschen die inneren, folglich wurde von außen nach innen geplant. Das Erscheinungsbild der hier geschaffenen Innenräume ist untergeordnet.

Um die Dünnhäutigkeit der Außenhaut zu betonen und der Plastizität der Kubusform entgegenzuwirken, geht der Putz der Außenwand nicht um die Ecke, sondern die Fensterleibungen sind aus Holz ausgebildet. Ich habe »den Kubus zerstört«, und zwar nicht durch räumliche Kontinuität, sondern durch die aus den örtlichen Gegebenheiten bedingten Verzerrungen.

To emphasize thinness of surface and contradict the plasticity of the form of the box, the stucco surface is detailed with a minimum of corner-turnings by means of the wood-surfaced window reveals. I have «destroyed the box», not through spatial continuities but by circumstantial distortions.

1. Gesamtansicht des Modells
2. Lageplan
3. Gesamtansicht der Eingangsfront

1. General view of the model
2. Site plan
3. General view of the access

4. Detail der Eckaussparung
5. Gesamtansicht
6. Erdgeschoß
7. Erstes Obergeschoß

4. Detail of the corner opening
5. General view
6. Ground floor
7. Second floor

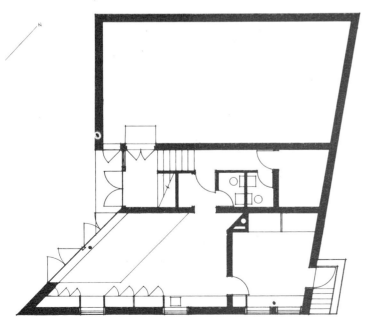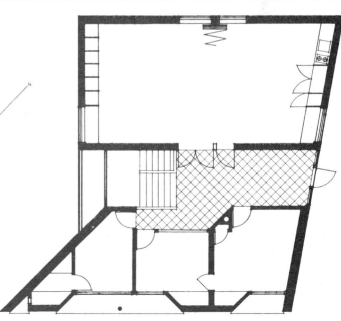

27

Wettbewerb für ein F. D. R. Denkmal, Washington, D.C., 1960
Robert Venturi, John Rauch, Nicholas Gionopulos

Es handelt sich hier um ein Geländerelief, das einen Kontrast bildet zu den in nächster Nähe bereits vorhandenen weißen Skulpturen der drei wichtigsten Gedenkstätten Washingtons und deren Wirkung dadurch verstärkt. Es ist aber keine vierte, an einem Parkplatz gelegene Skulptur. Es ist eine offene, weiße Marmorpromenade entlang des Potomac, die das Ufer des Flusses betont und für Fußgänger nutzbar macht; eine Straße, an der die Besucher parken können und die von schluchtähnlichen Mauern eingefaßt wird, wodurch sich ein Kontrast zu den umliegenden breiten Boulevards ergibt; auf der anderen Seite ist es ein grüner, grasbewachsener Hügel, der den Hintergrund für die am Wasserbecken stehenden Kirschbäume bildet. In der großen Krümmung des vertikalen Schnitts flußabwärts sind Rampen, Treppen und Passagen untergebracht. Ihre leicht strukturierte Oberfläche bietet von nahem ein interessantes Bild. Auf der anderen Seite ist die Oberfläche der durchgängigen Krümmung verschiedenartig gestaltet: Gras, bodenbedeckende Pflanzen, Weinstöcke und eine Betonkappe, die der Neigung der Krümmung entsprechend aufeinander folgen. Durch den Verlauf des offenen Parkgeländes bildet sich eine Vielzahl von Bereichen: die enge Fahrschlucht, die geschlossene Fußgängerpassage und die offene Promenade, die immer wieder von Elementen wie Bäumen oder Bänken durchbrochen wird.

1. Gesamtansicht
2. Grundriß und Ansicht
3. Perspektivischer Schnitt
4. Grundriß, Schnitt und Perspektiven übereinander

F.D.R. Memorial Competition, Washington, D.C., 1960
Robert Venturi, John Rauch, Nicholas Gionopulos

This is a directional earth form that contrasts and thereby enhances the white sculptural forms of the three mayor Washington memorials already existing in the neighborhood. It is not a fourth sculptural form next to a parking lot. It is several things at once: an open, white marble promenade along the Potomac, which recognizes and utilizes the river's edge for pedestrians; an integral street, which accommodates the visitors' parking and is enclosed by canyon-like walls contrasting with the open avenues around; and, on the other side, it is a green grass mound which is a background for the cherry trees on the basin. The complex curve of the vertical section on the riverside accommodates a multiplicity of ramps, stairs, and passages, and a surface in bas-relief, which is interesting close-up —yet by its extreme continuity, suggested and actual, this curve contributes a scale appropriately monumental and visible from a distance. On the other side the continous curve in section accommodates varying materials —grass, ground cover, vine, and concrete cap, in sequence and in relation to the varying degrees of the slope. A variety of spaces in afforded by the sequence of open park: tight vehicular canyon, close pedestrian passage, and open directional promenade, in turn relieved by details like trees and benches, and at the middle, on axis with the Washington obelisk, by a vision-slit spaned by a little vehicular bridge.

1. General perspective
2. Plan and elevation
3. Perpective-section
4. Superposition of plan, section and perspectives

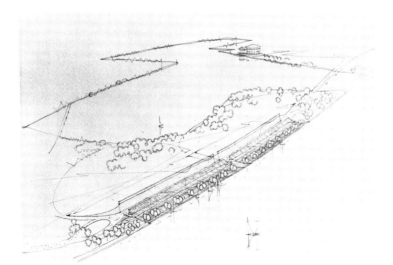
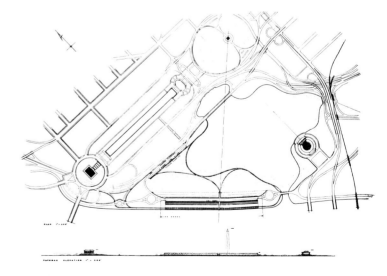

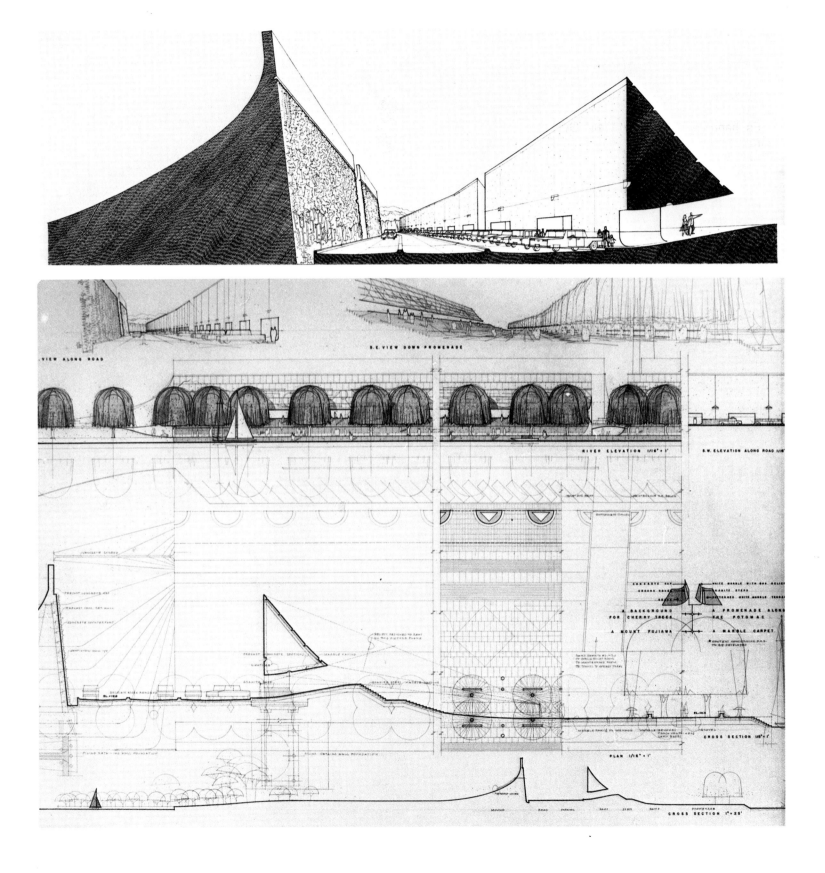

Umbau Grand's Restaurant, Philadelphia, Pennsylvania, 1961
Robert Venturi
Fotos: Lawrence Williams

Es handelt sich hier um den Umbau von zwei nebeneinander liegenden, baufälligen Reihenhäusern in ein bescheidenes Restaurant für Studenten der Umgebung. Dem Zweck und dem kleinen Budget entsprechend wurden durchweg konventionelle Mittel und Bauelemente verwendet, dies jedoch in einer Weise, daß alltägliche Elemente durch den geänderten Rahmen eine neue Bedeutung gewannen. So wurden zum Beispiel als Deckenleuchten große weiße Porzellanlampen des Typs R.L.M. verwendet – eine altmodische Industrielampe, die solide aber billig ist und die in diesem Zusammenhang elegant wirkt. Die Sitznischen entsprechen nicht den allgemein üblichen, übertrieben tiefen, gepolsterten

Grand's Restaurant Renovation, Philadelphia, Pennsylvania, 1961
Robert Venturi
Photography: Lawrence Williams

A renovation of two adjacent, dilapidated row houses into a modest neighborhood restaurant catering to students. In keeping with its purpose and the very modest budget conventional means and elements are used throughout, but in such a way as to make common things take on new meaning in their altered context. For example, for the main lighting fixtures are large-size white porcelain R.L.M.'s —an old fashioned industrial fixture that is solid but cheap and, in this context, elegant. The booths are designed not as the more common exaggeratedly low, upholstered types that expose the sitter, but as the more traditional, high kind with comfortable but modest padding and an appropriate sense of privacy. The wall ornamenta-

Ausführungen, in denen man sich wie auf dem Präsentierteller vorkommen muß, sondern eher der traditionellen Ausführung, das heißt, sie sind hochgeschlossen, haben eine bequeme, aber bescheidene Polsterung und schaffen eine angemessene Abgeschlossenheit. Als Wanddekoration wurden oberhalb der Sitznischenvertäfelung Muster direkt auf den Putz gemalt. An der Außenseite schließt in Höhe des ersten Obergeschosses ein emaillierter Schriftzug das Zusammenspiel von Dualität und Einheit ab. Die Tasse zieht die Blicke auf sich, wenn sie sich in den Augen des sich parallel zur Fassade nähernden Fußgängers von einer zwei- in eine dreidimensionale verwandelt. Nachts ist das Restaurant auffällig erleuchtet: dann erstrahlen die Buchstaben in durchsichtigem weißen Licht und die Tasse zeichnet sich in Neonlicht ab.

tion consists of painted patterns on the plaster above the wainscoting of the booths. On the exterior, the porcelain-enameled sign at the level of the second floor boldly concludes the play of duality and unity. The cup attracts the eye by envolving from two dimensions to three as pedestrians approach parallel to the façade. It is dramatically lit at night, with the letters becoming translucent white light and the cup outlined in neon.

1. Innenansicht
2. Blick von außen auf den Eingang
3. Innendetail

1. Interior view
2. Exterior view of the access
3. Interior Detail

Guild House, Wohnhaus für alte Menschen, Philadelphia, Pennsylvania, 1961
Robert Venturi
Mitarbeiter: Gerod Clark, Frank Kawasaki
Fotos: Frank Kawasaki, Steven Izenour

Auf einem kleinen städtischen Grundstück gelegen, birgt dieses sechsstöckige Gebäude 91 Wohnungen unterschiedlichen Zuschnitts für ältere Mieter, die in ihrer angestammten Umgebung wohnen bleiben wollten.

Das beschränkte Budget erforderte eine konventionelle Architektur, vor allem im Hinblick auf die Größe. Der Ziegel aus üblichem roten Ton paßt gut zu dem angrenzenden Lagerhaus. Längs des Gehsteigs wurden Ziegel anderer Größe verwendet als dort, wo die Straße bis an die Fassade herankommt. Die dunklen Wände mit ihren zweiteiligen Senkrechtschiebefenstern erinnern an traditionelle städtische Reihenhäuser, die Wirkung der Fenster jedoch ist wegen ihrer raffinierten Aufteilung ungewöhnlich – ungewöhnlich groß nämlich. Außerdem variiert die Größe der Fenster entsprechend ihren Abständen zur Straße.

Die Innenräume sind komplex, um den unterschiedlichen Erfordernissen des Raumprogramms für ein Appartementhaus zu entsprechen. Die Flure wurden minimiert, um ein Maximum an Nutzfläche zu erreichen.

Guild House. Friends Housing for the Elderly, Philadelphia, Pennsylvania, 1961
Robert Venturi
Collaborators: Gerod Clark, Frank Kawasaki
Photography: Frank Kawasaki, Steven Izenour

On a small urban site, this six-story building houses 91 apartments of varying types for elderly tenants who desired to remain in their old neighborhood.

Conventional architectural elements, particularly scale, were employed to accommodate budget constraints. The brick, an inexpresive red clay, matches an adjacent warehouse, but the brick nearest the sidewalk is of a different size from that used where the façade meets the street. The dark walls with double-hung windows recall traditional city row houses, but the effect of the windows is uncommon due to their subtle proportion —unusually big. The scale of the windows also differs according to their distance from the street.

Interior spaces are complex to suit the varied program of the apartment house. There is a maximum of interior volume and a minimun of corridor space.

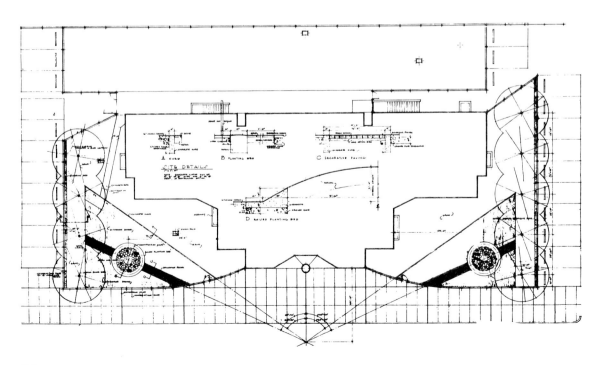

1. Grundriß
2. Blick von außen auf die Hauptfassade
3. Perspektive

1. General plan
2. Exterior view of the main façade
3. Perspective

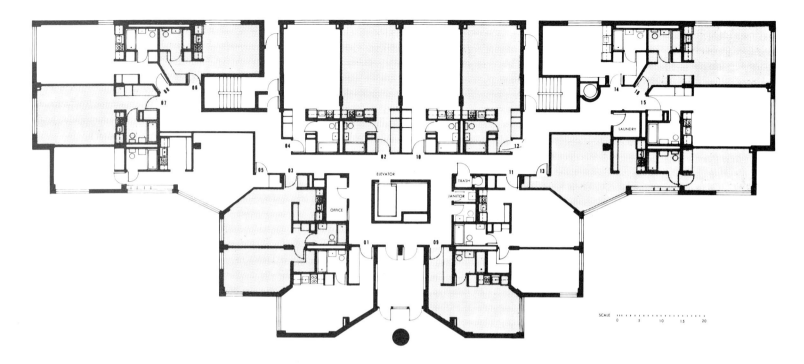

4. Erstes Obergeschoß
5. Drittes und viertes Obergeschoß
6. Innenansicht eines Schlafzimmers
7. Innenansicht des Zeichenraums im obersten Geschoß

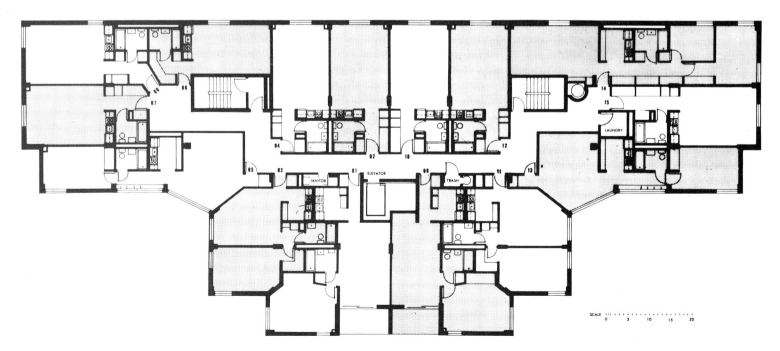

4. Second floor plan
5. Fourth and fifth floors, plans
6. Interior view of a bedroom
7. Interior view of the drawing room in the last floor

8. Innenansicht eines Raums
9. Gesamtansicht von außen

8. Interior view of a room
9. General exterior view

Haus Vanna Venturi, Chestnut Hill, Pennsylvania, 1962
Robert Venturi
Mitarbeiter: Arthur Jones
Fotos: Rollin La France, George Phol

Das Haus ist zugleich komplex und einfach, offen und geschlossen, groß und klein, seine Anordnung vereinigt die typischen Elemente eines Hauses im allgemeinen und die diesem Haus eigenen Elemente im speziellen. Sowohl außen wie innen ist es ein kleines Haus mit großzügigem Maßstab. Der Hauptgrund für diesen großen Maßstab war, ein Gegengewicht zu der Komplexität des Hauses zu schaffen – Komplexität in Verbindung mit kleinen Elementen in kleinen Gebäuden bedeutet Spannung.

Der Grundriß ist symmetrisch, jedoch wird diese Symmetrie gelegentlich verzerrt, um den speziellen Erfordernissen der Räume Rechnung zu tragen: Die Form der Küche auf der rechten Seite beispielsweise unterscheidet sich von der des Schlafzimmers auf der linken Seite. Zwei senkrechte Elemente – der offene Kamin und die Treppe – wetteifern um die zentrale Lage. Auf der einen Seite ist die Form der offenen Feuerstelle etwas verzerrt und zur Seite verschoben, ebenso der Kamin; auf der anderen Seite verengt die Treppe sich plötzlich wegen des Kamins und verändert ihren Verlauf.

Die äußere Form – in erster Linie bestimmt durch den oberen Wandabschluß und das Giebeldach – ist einfach und einheitlich und repräsentiert den Maßstab eines üblichen Hauses. Die Fassade mit ihrer konventionellen Anordnung von Tür, Fenstern, Schornstein und Giebel bildet das fast symbolische Bild eines Hauses. Die architektonische Vielfalt im

Vanna Venturi House, Chestnut Hill, Pennsylvania, 1962
Robert Venturi
Collaborator: Arthur Jones
Photography: Rollin La France, George Pohl

This building recognizes complexities and contradictions: it is both complex and simple, open and closed, big and little, its order accommodates the generic elements of a house in general, and the circumstantial elements of this house in particular. Inside and out, it is a little house with big scale. The main reason for the large scale is to counterbalance the complexity —complexity in combination with small in small buildings means busyness. The big scale in the small building achieves tension rather than nervousness.

The inside spaces are complex in their shapes and interrelationships, responding to the inherent domestic program as well as to some whimsies appropriate to an individual house. The plan is symmetrical, but the symmetry is distorted at times to accommodate the particular needs of the spaces: the kitchen on the right, for instance, varies from the bedroom on the left. Two vertical elements —the fireplace-chimney and the stair— compete, as it were, for central position. On one side the fireplace distorts in shape and moves over a little, as does its chimney; on the other side the stair suddenly constricts its width and changes its path because of the chimney.

The outside form —as represented by the parapeted wall and the gable roof— is simple and consistent it represents this house's public scale. The front, by its conventional combinations of door, windows, chimney and gable, creates an almost symbolic image of a house. However, the architectural com-

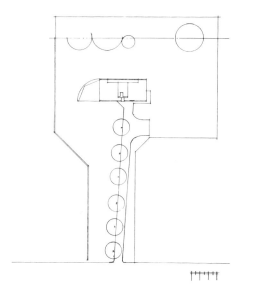

Innern des Hauses spiegelt sich jedoch auch an dessen Äußerem wider. Die unterschiedliche Anordnung der Fenster, ihre Größen und Formen, die Durchbrüche in den Außenwänden, wie auch der aus der Mitte seitlich verschobene Kamin stehen in einem Widerspruch zur Symmetrie der äußeren Form. Die Wände bilden Einschlüsse durch ihre schichtweise Anordnung, an der Vorder- und Rückseite jedoch sind sie aufgebrochen und vermitteln so eine Öffnung nach außen.

1. Gesamtansicht
2. Innenansicht auf den Kamin
3. Außenansicht der Hauptfassade

plexities inside are also reflected on the outside. The varying locations and sizes and shapes of the windows and perforations on the outside walls, as well as the off-center location of the chimney, contradict the overall symmetry of the exterior form. The walls are layered for enclosure yet punctured for openness in front and back. This occurs most vividly at the front center where the outside wall is superimposed upon the two other walls housing the stair. Each of these three layers juxtaposes openings of differing size and position. Here is layered space rather than interpenetrated space.

1. General plan
2. Interior view of the chimney
3. Exterior view of the main façade

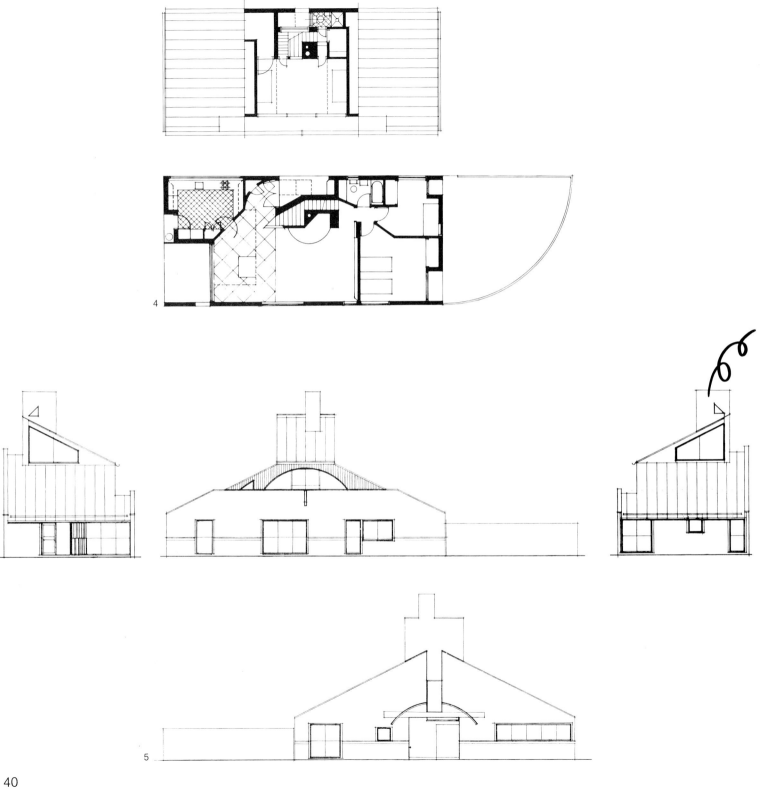

4. Erdgeschoß und erstes Obergeschoß
5. Fassaden
6. Außenansicht der rückwärtigen Fassade

4. Ground and second floors
5. Façades
6. Exterior view of the rear façade

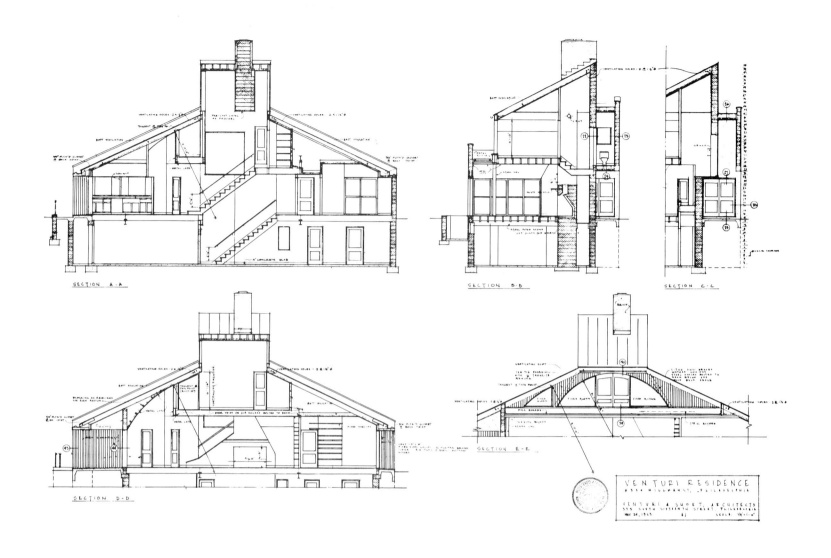

7. Sections and working details
8. Interior view of the dining room

9. Ausschnitt aus der Rückseite
10. Detail mit Haupteingang
11. Ausschnitt einer Innenansicht

9. Fragment of the rear façade
10. Detail of the front door
11. Interior detail

12. Detail der Hauptfassade
13. Innenansicht des Treppenraums

12. Detail of the main façade
13. Interior view of the staircase

Brunnen in Philadelphia, Pennsylvania, 1964
Robert Venturi, Denise Scott Brown
Mitarbeiter: Gerod Clark, Frank Kawasaki
Fotos: Rollin La France

Die Lage des Brunnens auf einem freigelassenen Block am Ende des Benjamin Franklin Parkway, die Gartenanlage und der Brunnendurchmesser von 27 m waren durch das Wettbewerbsprogramm vorgegeben.

Der mit 20 m höchste Wasserstrahl wird von einer Reihe von Quarzlampen angestrahlt und durch eine Metallschale, die innen konkav und außen konvex ist, vom Wind geschützt. Konstruiert ist diese Schale innen aus gebogenen Metallplanken, die verschweißt sind mit den äußeren Platten.

»Durch seine Größe und seine kühne Form hebt sich der Brunnen gegen die großen Gebäude im Hintergrund und das amorphe Umfeld ab. Seine plastische Form, seine gebogene Silhouette und seine glatte Oberfläche kontrastieren ebenfalls mit den vielfältigen rechteckigen Mustern der umliegenden Gebäude. Es sollte kein barocker Brunnen entstehen. Man nimmt ihn erst wahr, wenn man kurz davor steht oder von einem Auto aus, das im Verkehr steckengeblieben ist.«

Fountain in Philadelphia, Pennsylvania, 1964
Robert Venturi, Denise Scott Brown
Collaborators: Gerod Clark, Frank Kawasaki
Photography: Rollin La France

The location of the fountain within the open city block that terminates the Benjamin Franklin Parkway, as well as the garden's layout and the pond's diameter of 27 m. were all given by the Competition's program.

The main water jet, 20 m. high, is lighted with a series of quartz lams and protected from the wind by a metal shell which has a concave interior shape and a convex exterior shape. The structure is of bent plates inside, connected to the outer sheets at the welding points.

«The form is big and bold so that it will read against its background of big buildings and amorphous space. Its plastic shape, curving silhouette and plain surface also contrast with the intricate rectangular patterns of the buildings around. It was not meant to be a Baroque fountain to be read only close-up, or from a car stalled in traffic.»

1. Ansicht des Modells
2. Gesamtansicht. Fotomontage

1. View of the model
2. General view. Photomontage

Umbau der St. Francis de Sales-Kirche, Philadelphia, Pennsylvania, 1968
Robert Venturi
Mitarbeiter: John Anderson
Fotos: Stephen Hill

Nach der ökumenischen Bewegung änderten die Kirchen ihre Liturgie, so daß ein Umbau ihrer Altarräume notwendig wurde. Das Besondere an dieser Kirche sind ihre Einlegearbeiten aus Keramikfliesen sowie ihre marmornen und vergoldeten Mosaike. Wir schlugen vor, den Altarraum für die neue Zeremonie eher durch den Kontrast neu hinzugefügter Elemente als durch Analogie und Modifikation bestehender umzugestalten. Aus diesem Grund wählten wir Neonlicht und Kunststoff.

Der neue Altar, hinter dem der Priester jetzt mit dem Gesicht zur Gemeinde steht, ist seiner Form nach eher ein Tisch und nicht ein Sarkophag, wie es die alten Altäre waren. Er ist aus weißem, zirka 1,3 cm starkem Plexiglas, das abgekantet und durchsichtig ist. Als Beleuchtung wurde eine durchlaufende Neonlichtschlange gewählt, die an unsichtbaren Kabeln von der Decke hängt. Die Neonröhre in ihrer gebogenen Form durchläuft die gesamte Länge des Altarraums auf gleichbleibender Höhe.

Renovation of St. Francis de Sales Church, Philadelphia, Pennsylvania, 1968
Robert Venturi
Collaborator: John Anderson
Photography: Stephen Hill

After the ecumenical movement, churches changed their liturgy so that a renovation of their sanctuaries became necessary. At the same time, this church is characterized by the ceramic tile inlays, marble and gilded mosaics of its surfaces. The proposal was to accomodate the sanctuary to the new rituals through contrast and addition of new elements rather than analogy and modification of the existing fabric. This is why neon lights and plastic were chosen.

The new altar, which allows the priest to face the parishioners, has the shape of a table rather than the sarcophagus shape of the old altars. It is made of white folded half-inch translucent Plexiglas. The lighting consists of a continuous neon light line, suspended from the ceiling with invisible cables. This line, wich has a straight elevation and an undulating plan, runs the whole length of the altar space.

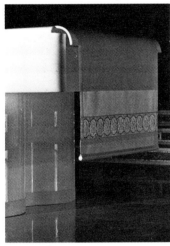

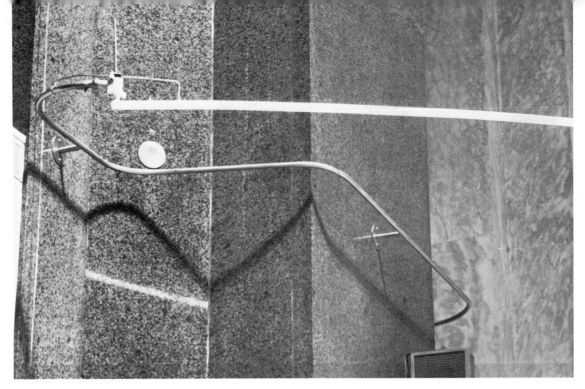

1. Gesamtansicht des Altars
2. Grundriß
3. Detail des Lesepults
4. Detail des Altars
5. Detail des Lehnstuhls
6. Detail des Neonlichts mit seiner Aufhängung
7. Aufhängung des Neonlichts

1. General view of the altar
2. Plan
3. Detail of the lectern
4. Detail of the altar
5. Detail of the armchair
6. Detail of the neon light with its support
7. Plan and elevations of the neon light support

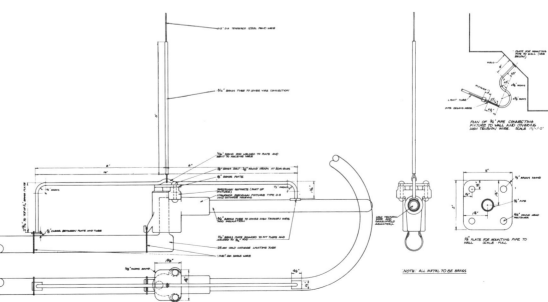

National College Hall of Fame, Wettbewerb, New Brunswick, New Jersey, 1967
Robert Venturi
Mitarbeiter: Gerod Clark, Frank Kawasaki
Fotos: George Phol

Das Programm für die College Football Hall of Fame verlangte eine präzise und gut durchdachte Aufteilung für Verwaltung, Forschung, Bibliothek und Speisesaal innerhalb der Ausstellungsflächen. Die Art der Ausstellung stand frei.

Der Entwurf vereint Projektion, Grafik und architektonischen Raum und schafft dadurch eine Medien-Ikonographie – um ein großes Publikum unterrichten, aber auch unterhalten zu können. Die Idee, daß ein Raum mittels Licht oder Bildern verwandelt werden kann, ist im Theater altbekannt, in der

National College Hall of Fame Competition, New Brunswick, New Jersey, 1967
Robert Venturi
Collaborators: Gerod Clark, Frank Kawasaki
Photography: George Pohl

The program for the College Football Hall of Fame called for precise and elaborate relationship for administrative, research, library and dining facilities within the exhibition spaces. The method of display was unrestricted.

The design combined projection, graphics and traditional architectural space to create a media iconography —to teach as well as entertain a large audience. This idea, that a space can be transformed by light and pictures, is an old one in the theater, but a relatively recent concept in architecture.

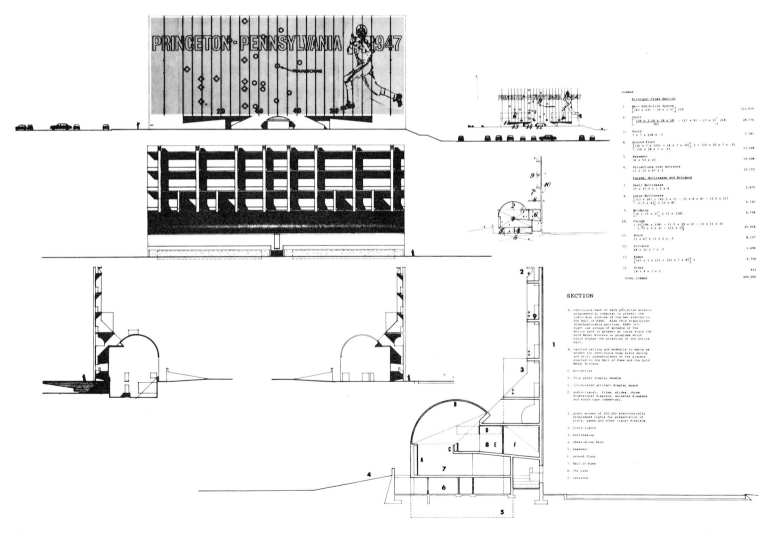

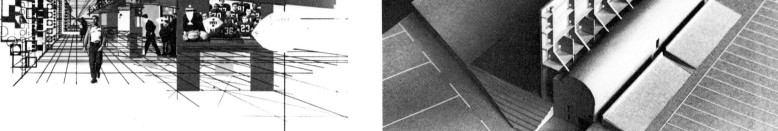

Architektur aber ein relativ neues Konzept.

Das Programm ist auf einen hohen Grad an Interaktion ausgelegt. Bilder der ganz großen Momente in der Geschichte des College-Footballs werden auf die Innenwände projiziert. Eine reichhaltige Mischung der Symbolik und Formensprache wurde benutzt, um die mitreißende Wirkung des Sports zu wiederholen. Das Äußere des Gebäudes wirkt wie ein Ankunftsort, um die Erwartungen der Besucher zu steigern. An der Rückseite des Gebäudes liegt die Haupttribüne, ausgerichtet auf das Hall of Fame Football-Feld.

1. Fassaden und Schnitte
2. Perspektive des Innenraums, Collage
3. Gesamtansicht der Hauptfassade, Modell
4. Gesamtansicht der Rückseite des Modells

The scheme emphasized a high degree of interaction. Films of great moments in college football history were projected over the interior surface. A rich mix of motion and changing scale was used to recreate the excitement of the sport. The exterior of the building was designed to create an arrival sequence which heightened the tourist's sense of anticipation. The rear of the building was integrated with a grandstand facing the Hall of Fame Football Field.

1. Elevations and sections
2. Perspective-collage of the interior
3. General view of the main façade, model
4. General vear view of the model

Städtisches Verwaltungszentrum in Thousand Oaks, Wettbewerb, Thousand Oaks, California, 1969
Robert Venturi
Mitarbeiter: Steven Izenour, Tony Pett, John Anderson, W. G. Clark, James Greifendorf, Denise Scott Brown

Dieses Projekt war ein Wettbewerbsbeitrag für ein Rathaus und eine Handelskammer auf einem vorstädtischen, kalifornischen Hügelgelände oberhalb des Ventura Freeway. Der Entwurf vereinigt die typischen Merkmale einer amerikanischen Vorstadtgegend; es werden Zeichen und Symbole verwendet, die selbst bei großer Geschwindigkeit über die Weite der Landstraße hinweg wahrgenommen werden können und die sich auf den Namen der Gemeinde sowie auf die traditionelle Rathaus-Architektur beziehen. Die Gebäude und Parkplätze wurden in ihrer Form dem Gelände angepaßt und schneiden somit minimal in die Landschaft ein.

Die Gebäudeteile des Rathauses bestehen aus einheitlichen Konstruktionsmodulen, ausgelegt auf ein Maximum an Flexibilität und Erweiterungsmöglichkeiten, dem stark betonten Eingang zum Sitzungssaal und einem Turm, der die für diese Gegend typischen Eichen symbolisieren soll. Tagsüber nimmt man den Baumturm kaum vor seinem Hintergrund wahr, nachts jedoch erstrahlt er im Neonlicht und hebt sich, klein aber hell, vor der dunklen Hügellandschaft ab.

Thousand Oaks Civic Center Competition, Thousand Oaks, California, 1969
Robert Venturi
Collaborators: Steven Izenour, Tony Pett, John Anderson, W.G. Clark, James Greifendorf, Denise Scott Brown

This project was a design competition for a City Hall and Chamber of Commerce on a suburban California hillside overlooking the Ventura Freeway. The design incorporated the symbols of the American suburban landscape, using signs and symbols that could be perceived at high speeds across the vast spaces of the highway, and that related to the name of the community and the traditional architecture of town halls. The buildings and parking areas were designed to follow the contours of the rolling site, causing minimum intrusion on the landscape.

The City Hall building consists of units of modular construction, designed for maximum flexibility and growth, and a ceremonial entrance to the council chamber, a tower symbolizing the live oak native to this area. By day, the tree tower is only lightly defined against its background; by night, the live oak is etched in neon, standing out small but bright against the dark hillside.

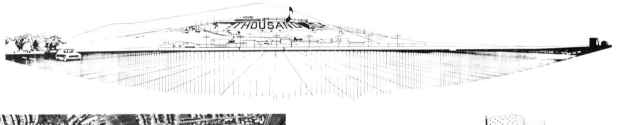

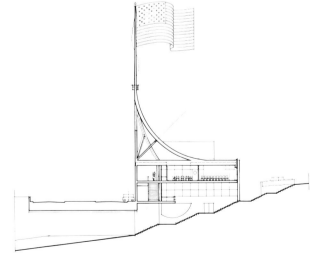

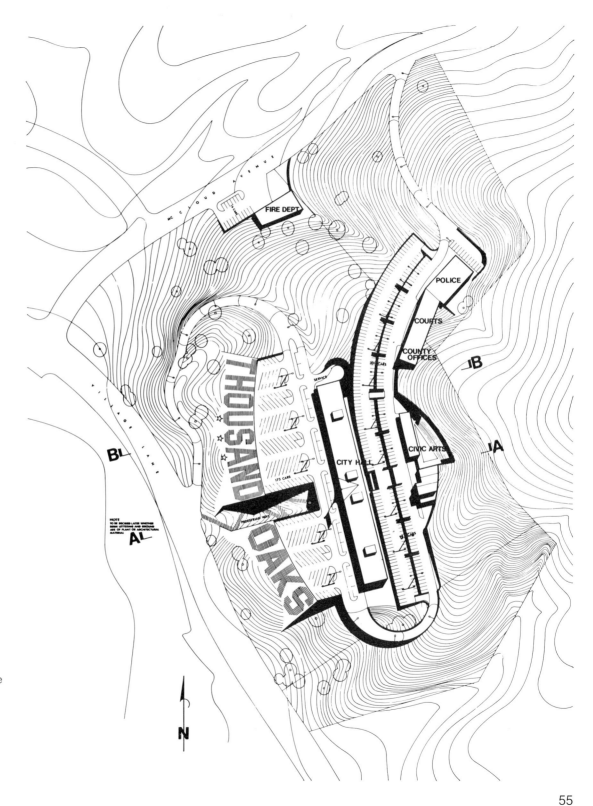

1. Gesamtansicht
2. Gelände aus der Vogelperspektive
3. Querschnitt
4. Lageplan

1. General perspective
2. Bird's eye view of the site
3. Crosswise section
4. Site plan

Fakultätsclub, Pennsylvania State University, University Park, Pennsylvania, 1974
Robert Venturi, John Rauch
Projektleiter: Robert Renfro
Mitarbeiter: Janet Colesberry, Missy Maxwell, Dick Rice
Fotos: Stephen Shore, Tom Bernard

Inmitten eines Eichenwäldchens gelegen, erinnert der Penn State Faculty Club an ein geräumiges, vorstädtisches Schindeldachhaus aus den 20er Jahren. Ein Anliegen der Universität war es, das Gebäude mit dem benachbarten Nittany Lion Inn, einem im neugeorgianischen Stil erbauten Gebäude, in einen harmonischen Einklang zu bringen, daher wirkt sein Äußeres weder kommerziell noch institutionell. Statt dessen wurde dem Gebäude ein »weiches«, beinahe häusliches, aber auch würdiges Erscheinungsbild gegeben. Die Innengestaltung ist den traditionellen Bankettsälen englischer mittelalterlicher Universitäten nachempfunden – einer langen Halle mit einer hohen gotischen Fensterfassade. Die Ausführung ist eine zeitgenössische Variante davon, um dem Club eine symbolische Tradition zu verleihen. In dem Gebäude sind ein Speisesaal, Küche und Versorgungsräume, eine Bar und Aufenthaltsräume untergebracht.

Faculty Club. Pennsylvania State University, University Park, Pennsylvania, 1974
Robert Venturi, John Rauch
Project Director: Robert Renfro
Collaborators: Janet Colesberry, Missy Maxwell, Dick Rice
Photography: Stephen Shore, Tom Bernard

Reminiscent of a spacious, shingled suburban house of the 1920s, the Penn State Faculty Club sits comfortably in a grove of oaks. In order to accommodate the University's concern about the new building's relationship to the adjacent Nittany Lion Inn, a Georgian Revival building, the appearance of the building is neither commercial nor institutional. Instead, a «soft», domestic, but also dignified image was sought for this building where faculty go to relax, dine and entertain their guests.

The interior plan is derived from the traditional banqueting hall of English medieval universities —a long, narrow hall building with a high arched Gothic window façade. This approach was adapted into more contemporary forms to give a symbolic tradition to the Club. The building includes dining facilities for 100, kitchen and service areas, a bar, lounge areas, and meeting rooms.

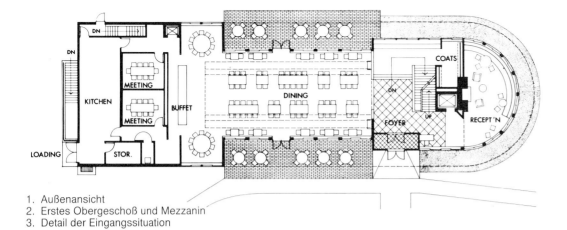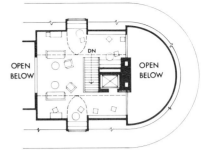

1. Außenansicht
2. Erstes Obergeschoß und Mezzanin
3. Detail der Eingangssituation

1. General exterior view
2. Second floor and mezzanine
3. Detail of the access

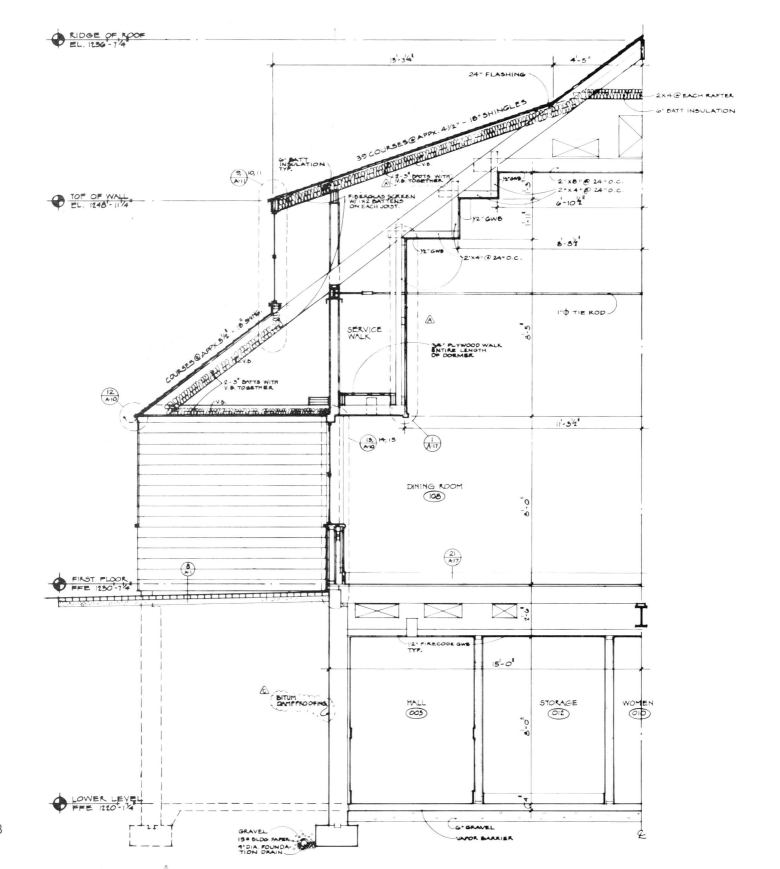

4. Ausführungsplan, Schnitt
5. Teilansicht der Hauptfassade
6. Innenansicht des Speisesaals

4. Construction section
5. Fragment of the main façade
6. Interior view of the dining room

Haus Lieb, Loveladies, New Jersey, 1967
Robert Venturi
Mitarbeiter: Gerod Clark

Es ist leicht zu sagen, was das Haus Lieb nicht ist: Es ist kein geschmackvoller, holzverkleideter Bau aus komplexen und widersprüchlichen Flügeln und Satteldach. Es ist ein gewöhnliches Haus, das aus gebräuchlichen Elementen besteht. Es hat eine Verkleidung aus Asbestzementschindeln mit einer holzähnlichen Oberflächenstruktur; Holz war einst das für Long Beach Island typische Baumaterial. Das Haus besteht aus großen Elementen, wie zum Beispiel die Treppe, die zunächst die ganze Breite des Hauses einnimmt und sich dann langsam auf eine Breite von 1,20 m im ersten Obergeschoß verjüngt. Die verwendeten nicht alltäglichen Bauelemente sind in ihrem Erscheinungsbild extrem ungewöhnlich, wie zum Beispiel das große runde Fenster, das aussieht wie der Lautsprecher eines Radios in den 30er Jahren. Es ist ein kleines Haus mit großem Maßstab, und es verleugnet nicht seine von Lichtleitungsmasten bestimmte Umgebung.

Lieb House, Loveladies, New Jersey, 1967
Robert Venturi
Collaborator: Gerod Clark

It is easy to explain what the Lieb House is not: It is not a tasteful, natural-wood-shingled configuration of complex and contradictory wings and shed roofs. It is an ordinary shed with conventional elements. It uses asbestos shingles with imitation wood-grain relief, once the indigenous building material on Long Beach Island. And it uses big elements, such as the stair that starts out the width of the house and gradually decreases to three feet on the second floor. Its unconventional elements are explicity extraordinary when they do occur, as in the big round window that looks like a 1930s radio loud-speaker. It is a little house with big scale, different from the houses around it but also like them. It tries not to make the plaster madonna in the birdbath next door look silly, and it stands up to, rather than ignores, the environment of utility poles.

1. Detail der Eingangssituation
2. Gesamtansicht der Rückseite
3. Gesamtansicht der Hauptfassade

1. Detail of the access
2. General rear view
3. General view of the main façade

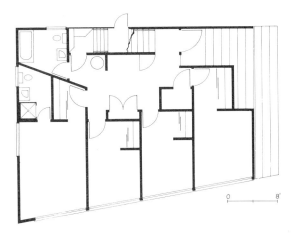
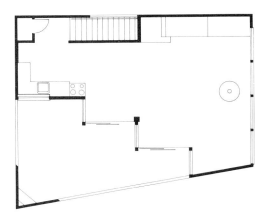

4. Innenansicht des Wohnraums
5. Grundriß zweites Obergeschoß
6. Grundriß erstes Obergeschoß
7. Das Haus und seine Umgebung

4. Interior view of the living-room
5. Third floor plan
6. Second floor plan
7. The house and its surroundings

Haus Hersey, Projekt, Hyannis Port, Massachusetts, 1968
Robert Venturi

Dem Entwurf für ein Sommerstrandhaus für eine kleine Familie am Cape Cod liegt unsere Idee des dekorierten Schuppens zugrunde. Dem Budget entsprechend entstand ein einfacher Kubus aus Asbestzementplatten mit einem Flachdach und einer Rückseite im sprichwörtlichen Schema »F«. Die Veranda an der Vorderseite ist dekoriert, um die Fassade größer erscheinen zu lassen. Die kreisförmige Öffnung, suggeriert durch den Rundbogen oder das Spalier ober- und das Geländer unterhalb, läßt die seitlichen Fassaden abgerückt erscheinen und umfaßt beide Geschosse – der großzügigen Ordnung einer klassischen Vorhalle entsprechend.

Hersey House. Project, Hyannis Port, Massachusetts, 1968
Robert Venturi

This design for a summer beach cabin for a small family on Cape Cod is the firm's most literal decorated shed. To satisfy the budget, it is a simple box of asbestos shingles with a flat roof and the proverbial «Mary Anne» behind. Ornament is applied to the front porch to increase the scale of the façade. The circular opening, suggested by the curve or the lattice above and the rail below, extends beyond the sides of the façade and includes both stories —like the giant order on a Classical porch. The goal was to achieve a poignant shed, both little and big, ordinary and sophisticated.

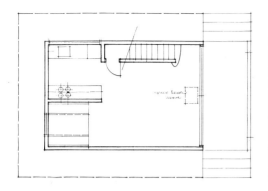
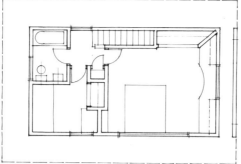
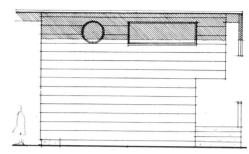

1. Gesamtansicht der rückwärtigen Fassade des Modells
2. Grundriß Erdgeschoß
3. Grundriß erstes Obergeschoß
4. Seitliche Ansicht
5. Ansicht der Hauptfassade, Modell

1. General rear view of the model
2. Ground floor plan
3. Second floor plan
4. Side elevation
5. View of the main façade, model

Haus D'Agostino, Projekt, Clinton, New York, 1968
Robert Venturi
Mitarbeiter: W. G. Clark

Dieses Haus, entworfen für ein ländliches Grundstück, sollte vielfältige Blickmöglichkeiten auf die umliegende schöne Hochebene im nördlichen Teil des Staates New York bieten. Aus diesem Grund wurde die Hauptebene um ein halbes Geschoß über das vorhandene Niveau angehoben. Das Haus ist aus grau glasierten Backsteinen, um sich farblich den verwitterten Brettern der nahegelegenen Scheune anzupassen. Die Fassade, von der langen Zufahrtsstraße aus gesehen, bildet eine ausdrucksvolle Silhouette und erinnert mit ihrem stufenförmigen oberen Wandabschluß an holländische Architektur.

Der Pavillon am Ende des Schwimmbeckens ist eine Parodie auf das große Haus. Das Schlafzimmer im Obergeschoß ist ein Holzgewölberaum – den polnischen Synagogen des 18. Jahrhunderts nachempfunden.

D'Agostino House. Project, Clinton, New York, 1968
Robert Venturi
Collaborator: W.G. Clark

This house, planned for a rural site, was to provide varied views surrounding a beautiful plateau in northern New York State. For this reason the main floor is raised half a level above grade. The house is made of gray-glazed brick to match the color of the weathered planks of a nearby barn. The façade toward the long approach forms a bold silhouette with a stepped parapet reminiscent of Dutch architecture. The bold scale must accommodate the automobile as well, because the garage is the usual entrance in this snowy climate. Rather than via a mean garage into a back door to the kitchen, you enter through a «beautiful» garage onto a «grand» stairway and up to the piano nobile, as if from the carriage-way of an 18th-century Neapolitan villa.

The pavilion at the end of the pool is a small parody of the big house. The bedroom on the top floor is vaulted in wood — like the Polish synagogues of the eighteenth century.

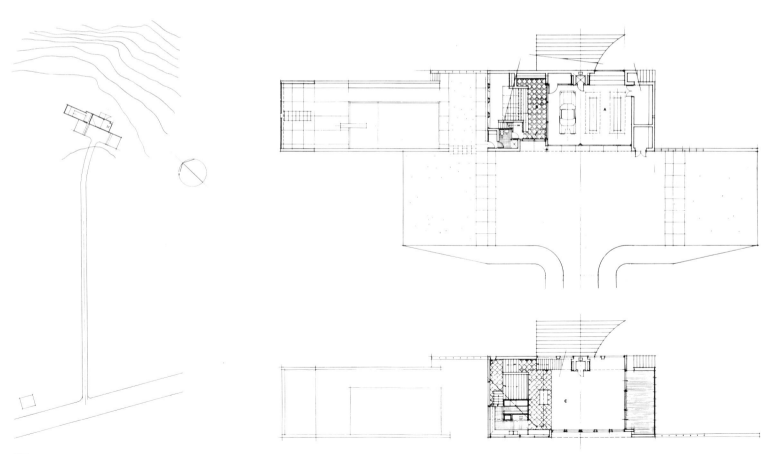

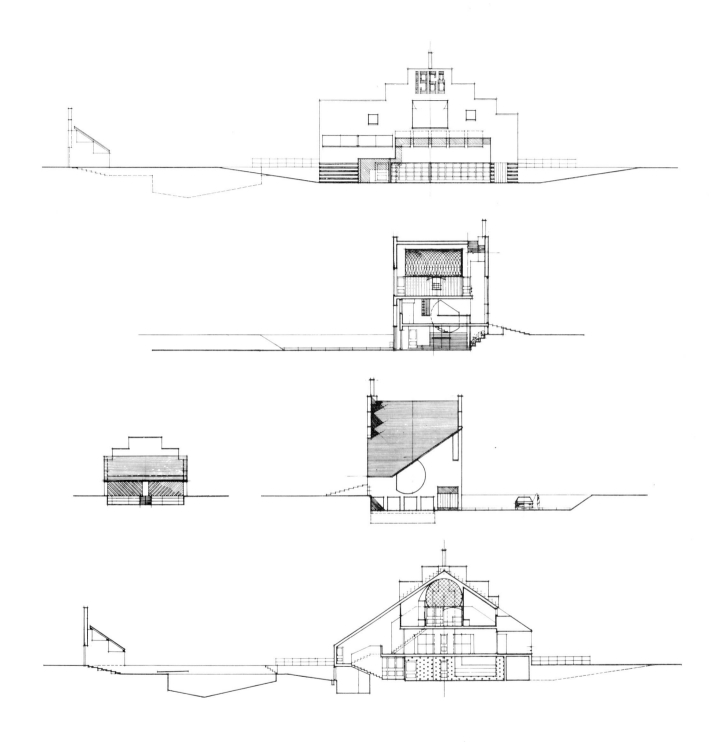

1. Lageplan	5. Querschnitt
2. Grundriß Erdgeschoß	6. Seitenansicht
3. Grundriß erstes Obergeschoß	7. Längsschnitt
4. Ansicht der Rückseite	

1. Site plan	5. Crosswise section
2. Ground floor plan	6. Side elevations
3. Second floor plan	7. Lengthwise section
4. Rear elevation	

Mathematische Fakultät, Wettbewerb, Yale University, New Haven, Connecticut, 1969
Robert Venturi
Mitarbeiter: W. G. Clark, Steven Izenour, Denise Scott Brown, Doug Southworth, David Vaughan

Unter 475 abgegebenen Vorschlägen des landesweiten Wettbewerbs gewann dieser Entwurf für einen fünfgeschossigen Ziegelanbau an die Leet-Oliver Hall den ersten Preis.

Das Gebäude der Mathematischen Fakultät von Yale erinnert an gotische Fassadengestaltung und gleichzeitig an öffentliche Gebäude der jüngsten Vergangenheit. Seine Monumentalität liegt darin, die umliegenden Gebäude besser zur Geltung zu bringen. Das Gebäude wurde in einem großzügigen Maßstab entworfen, seine massige Form wirkt aber eher klein durch die verkürzte Straßenfassade, das zurückgesetzte obere Geschoß, den Farbwechsel im dritten Obergeschoß und nicht zuletzt durch seinen abgewinkelten Grundriß – was für seine Stellung gegenüber der Leet-Oliver Hall von Bedeutung ist.

Das harmonische Nebeneinander der beiden Gebäude wird aber auch durch Kontraste unterstrichen. Die Fenstertypen sind unterschiedlich, deren Größen aber ähnlich; das Baumaterial ist unterschiedlich geartet und strukturiert, in der Farbe aber ähnlich. Auf der Rückseite unterscheidet sich das Pflastermuster der Plaza und die Verblendung des Eingangs in Größe und Material von der Leet-Oliver-Ornamentik, ähnelt ihr aber in der Symbolik.

Yale Mathematics Building Competition, Yale University, New Haven, Connecticut, 1969
Robert Venturi
Collaborators: W.G. Clark, Steven Izenour, Denise Scott Brown, Doug Southworth, David Vaughan

This proposed five-story brick addition to Leet-Oliver Hall was the winning submission among 475 entries in a national competition.

The design of the Yale Mathematics Building calls to mind both Gothic decoration and the institutional building of the recent past. Its monumentality lies in its ability to enhance the building around it. A large scale is maintained while its bulk is diminished by a shortened street façade, the set back at the upper floor, the change of color value at the fourth floor, and by inflection in the shape of the plan —important in its relation to Leet-Oliver Hall.

Harmony with Leet-Oliver is also achieved through contrast. The windows are different in type yet similar in scale; the material is different in type and texture yet similar in color. At the back, the paving pattern of the plaza and the tracery of the entrance are different in both scale and material from the ornament of Leet-Oliver, yet similar symbolically.

1. Lageplan
2. Perspektive
3. Grundriß erstes Obergeschoß
4. Untergeschoß
5. Nord-West-Ansicht

1. Site Plan
2. Perspective
3. Second floor plan
4. Basement floor
5. N.W. Elevation

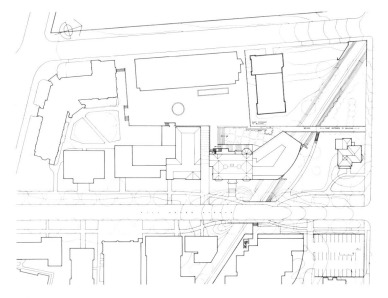

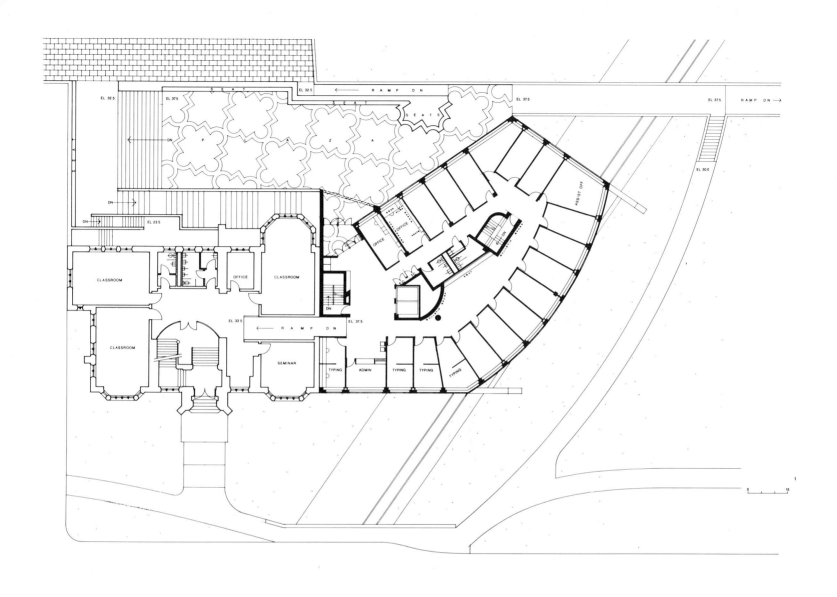
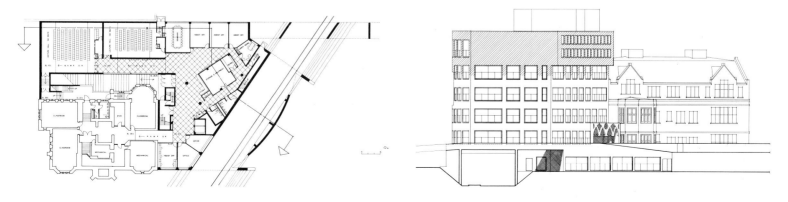

69

Trubek-Wislocki Häuser, Nantucket Island, Massachusetts, 1970
Robert Venturi
Projektleiter: Terry Vaughan
Fotos: Steven Izenour

Die zwei Ferienhäuser, die für einen Yale-Professor und dessen Familie sowie für Verwandte erbaut wurden, liegen in einem Moorgebiet in Nantucket, direkt am Meer. Das größere Haus ist komplex und widersprüchlich, das kleinere ist eher alltäglich. Die Häuser sind zum Meer ausgerichtet. Zunächst von der Rückseite betrachtet, wirken sie weit genug voneinander entfernt, um sie unabhängig voneinander wirken zu lassen, aber immer noch so nah, um sie als Paar wahrzunehmen. Sie passen gut in die Umgebung, denn in gewisser Hinsicht ähneln sie den alten Fischerhütten auf der Insel, aber auch den Schindel-Ferienhäusern im Neu-England des 19. Jahrhunderts – grau verwittert, um mit dem graugrünen Laub und dem sanft blauen Meer zu verschmelzen.

Trubek-Wislocki Houses, Nantucket Island, Massachusetts, 1970
Robert Venturi
Project Director: Terry Vaughan
Photography: Steven Izenour

These are two vacation cottages on a moor by the sea in Nantucket for a Yale professor and his family and for a related family. The larger house is complex and contradictory; the smaller house is more ordinary. The houses are sited so as to look toward the water. First seen from the rear, they are set far enough apart to create a sense of openness, yet close enough to be perceived as a pair. They fit into the environment because they are like the old fishermen's cottages of that island in some ways and like 19th century shingle style vacation houses of New England too —weathered grey to meld into the grey-green foliage and soft blue seascape.

1. Gesamtansicht der beiden Häuser
2. Innenansicht Haus Trubek

1. General view of the two houses
2. Interior view of Trubek house

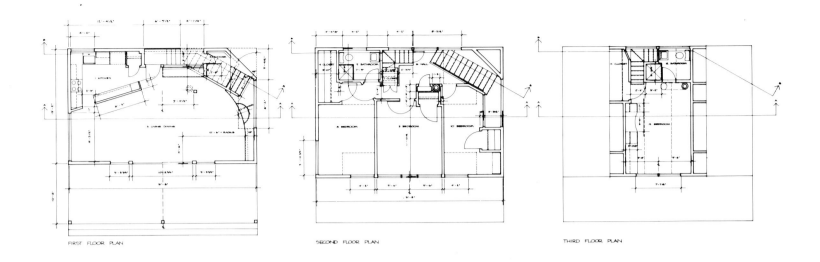
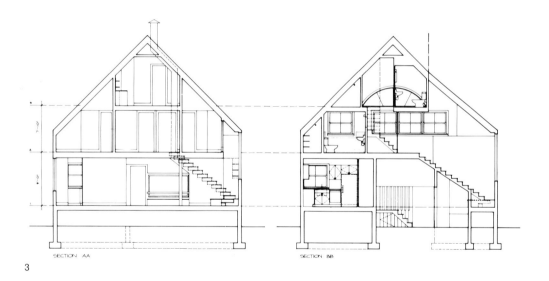

3. Grundrisse und Schnitte Haus Trubek
4. Ansichten Haus Trubek
5. Innenansicht des Wohn- und Eßraums Haus Trubek

3. Plans and sections of Trubek house
4. Elevations of Trubek house
5. Interior view of the living-dining room of Trubek house

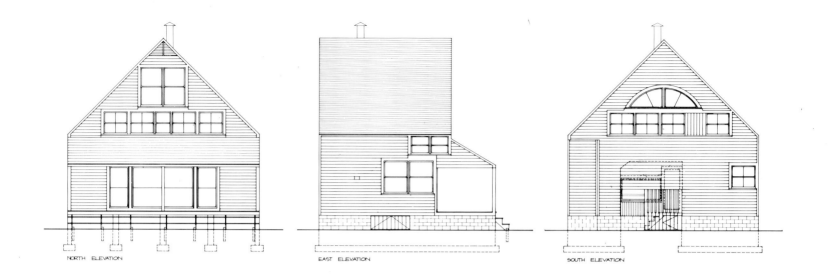

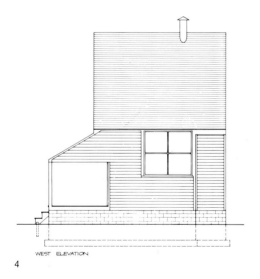

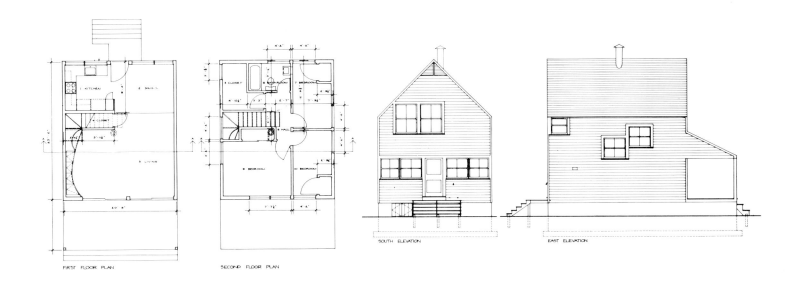
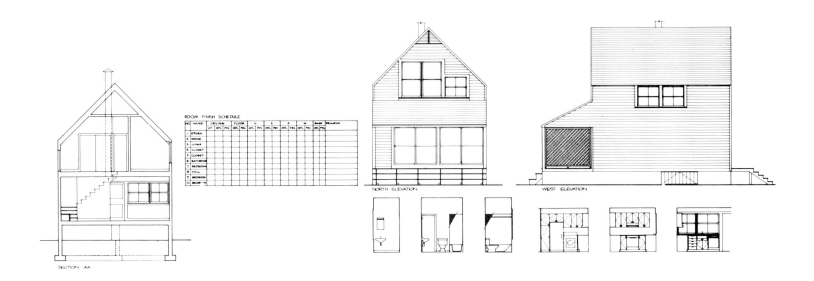

6. Grundrisse, Schnitte und Ansichten Haus Wislocki
7. Außenansicht Haus Wislocki

6. Plans, section and elevations of Wislocki house
7. Exterior view of Wislocki house

Franklin Court, Philadelphia, Pennsylvania, 1972
Robert Venturi
Projektleiter: David Vaugham
Mitarbeiter: Stanford Hughes, Missy Maxwell, Robert Renfro, Dick Rice, Denis Scott Brown, Terry Vaughan

Die Gedenkstätte für Benjamin Franklin liegt auf dem Grundstück, auf dem einst Franklins Haus stand, im historischen Altstadtkern von Philadelphia. Das Museum sollte sich in seine Umgebung einfügen, aber auch seine eigene Identität haben. Um diesen verschiedenen Anforderungen gerecht zu werden, gingen wir von der normalen Museums- und Gedenkstätten-Architektur aus, verlegten die eigentliche Ausstellungsfläche unter die Erde und stellten eine »Phantom«-Konstruktion aus Stahl auf, die der Form des ursprünglichen Hauses entsprach. Sichtluken erlauben den Besuchern einen Blick auf die wenigen archäologischen Zeugnisse des Hauses, die bei früheren Untersuchungen des Geländes zum Vorschein gekommen waren. Zitate aus Briefen, die Franklin während des Hausbaus an seine Frau geschrieben hatte, sind im Pflaster eingemeißelt.

Franklin Court, Philadelphia, Pennsylvania, 1972
Robert Venturi
Project Director: David Vaugham
Collaborators: Stanford Hughes, Missy Maxwell, Robert Renfro, Dick Rice, Denise Scott Brown, Terry Vaughan

This project, a museum and memorial to Benjamin Franklin, is on the site of the home Franklin built for himself, set back from Market Street in the historic Old City in Philadelphia. The museum needed to fit into its context, yet have a distintive identity of its own. It was to serve educational and memorial purposes, stimulate its visitors' imaginations, convey a rich history, and reflect Franklin's spirit as well as tell the story of his life and accoplishments.

The response to these multiple challenges departed from usual museum and memorial architecture by placing the main exhibit area underground and designing a steel «ghost» structure to represent the original house. This preserved as open space the site of Franklin's garden. Viewing ports are provided to allow visitors to see the few archeological remains of the house uncovered during earlier research on the property. Quotes from Franklin's letters to his wife during the house's construction are engraved in the paving.

1. Ansicht der zum Platz ausgerichteten Vorhalle
2. Gesamtansicht

1. View of the porch facing the square
2. General view

Haus Brant, Greenwich, Connecticut, 1970
Robert Venturi
Verantwortliche Architekten: Gerod Clark, Arthur Jones
Mitarbeiter: Paul Hirshorn, Anthony Pellecchia, Terry Vaughan
Fotos: Cervin Robinson

Das Haus wurde für ein junges Paar gebaut, das seine Sammlung von Pop Art-Gemälden und Art Deco-Objekten unterbringen wollte.

Die Südfassade weist eine kontrapunktische Rhythmik von Türen und Fenstern auf und erinnert an ein einfaches georgianisches Landhaus, aber die in zwei Grüntönen glasierten Backsteine bewirken ins Auge fallende Op Art/Art Deco-Muster. Im Gegensatz dazu hat die andere ungemusterte Seite des Hauses ein zentrales Motiv, und der Rhythmus der hier größeren Öffnungen ist komplexer, um die größere Höhe und die großen Innenräume widerzuspiegeln.

Der Haupteingang zu dem Haus erfolgt über eine flache, ausladende Treppe, die vom abgesenkten Autostellplatz mit Zugang zu einem offenen Untergeschoß und einer Doppelgarage nach oben führt in eine lange, zweigeschossige Galerie, in der einige der großformatigen Gemälde der Sammlung hängen. Diese Galerie öffnet sich zu einem Garten im Norden, zu einer Reihe von Zimmern im Süden und zu einer Treppe, die ins erste Obergeschoß führt. An der Südseite der Galerie liegt die Küche, von der aus das Spielzimmer und die Bibliothek eingesehen werden können.

Brant House, Greenwich, Connecticut, 1970
Robert Venturi
Architects in Charge: Gerod Clark, Arthur Jones
Collaborators: Paul Hirshorn, Anthony Pellecchia, Terry Vaughan
Photography: Cervin Robinson

A house constructed for a young couple who wanted to house their collection of Por Art paintings and Art Deco objects and accommodate their growing family. The site is 30 acres, serenely beautiful, flat, open and lightly wooded.

The south elevation has a contrapuntal rhythm of doors and windows recalling a plain Georgian country house, but the green glazed brick in two shades makes a bold Op Art/Art Deco pattern. In contrast, the other side of the house, unpatterned, has a central motif and a more complex rhythm of openings with a bigger scale to reflects its greater height and the large inside spaces.

The main entrance to the house is a low flight of wide stairs leading upward from a sunken auto court with access to an open basement and two-car garage. The stairs lead into a long two-story gallery displaying some of the big paintings in the collection. This gallery opens on a garden toward the north a series of rooms to the south, and the stairs to the second floor. On the south side of the gallery, the kitchen is arranged to oversee the children's playroom on one side and the library on the other, where the family can eat informally.

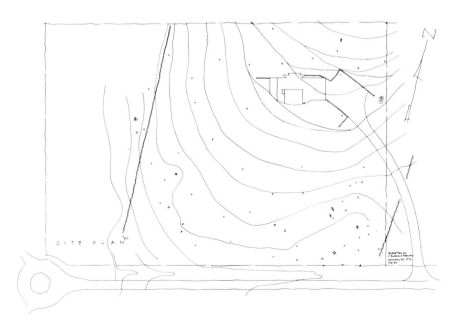

1. Lageplan
2. Grundriß und Ausführungsdetai
3. Grundriß erstes Obergeschoß

1. Site plan
2. Ground floor and working detail
3. Second floor plan

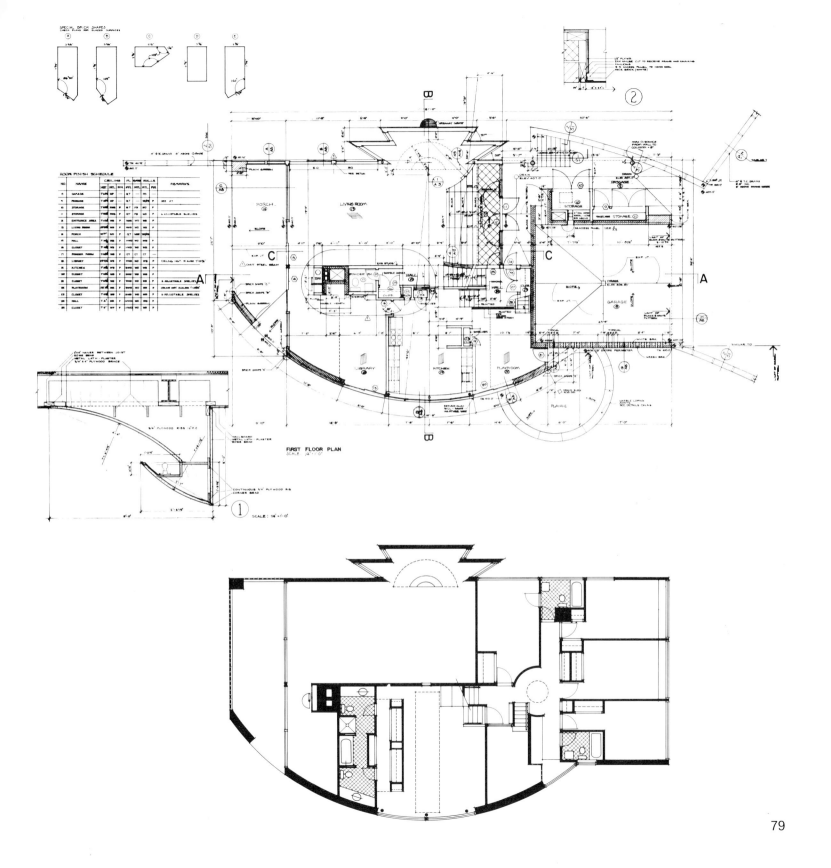

4. Ansicht der Hauptfassade   4. Exterior view of the main façade

5. Ansicht der Rück- und Seitenfassade

5. Exterior view of the rear and side façades

6. Studie der Hauptfassade
7. Fassadenausschnitt
8. Innenansicht der Halle
9. Blick in die Garagen-Vorhalle
10. Gesamtansicht

6. Study of the main elevation
7. Façade detail
8. Interior view of the hall
9. View of the garage-porch
10. General view

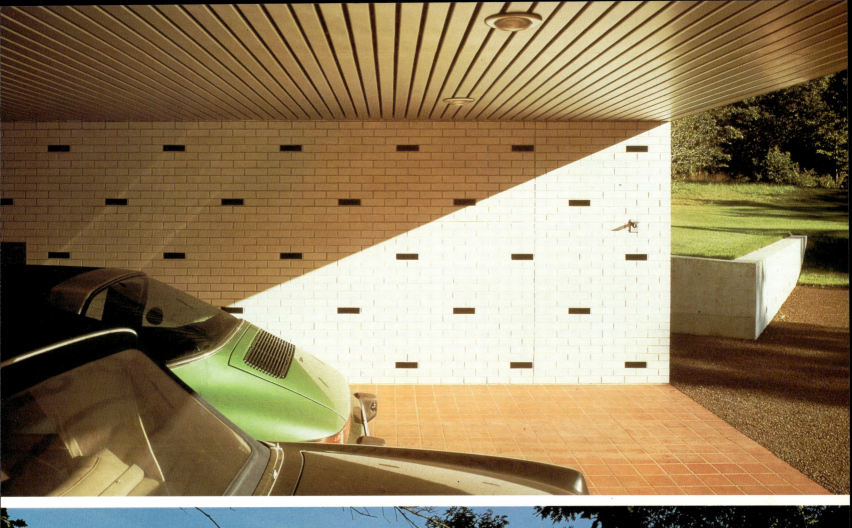

11. Innenansicht vom Eßzimmer aus
12. Eßzimmer

11. Interior view from dining room level
12. Interior view of the dining room

Umbau des Allen Memorial Art Museum, Oberlin College, Ohio, 1973

Robert Venturi, John Rauch
Verantwortlicher Architekt: Jeffery Ryan
Mitarbeiter: Tony Atkin, Janet Colesberry, Stanford Hughes, Dick Rice, Denise Scott Brown
Fotos: Collin Tom Bernard

Um den Anbau auf der schmalen Fläche des Grundstücks unterzubringen, wurde er asymmetrisch an das bestehende Gebäude angefügt. Dabei war besonders darauf zu achten, eine harmonische Einheit zwischen dem Anbau und dem symmetrischen Renaissance-Pavillon von Cass Gilbert herzustellen. Dies geschah aber nicht etwa durch eine Imitation des Pavillons, sondern durch die Abstimmung verschiedener Materialien – gelbbrauner Backstein, roter Sandstein und rosafarbener Granit, mit denen ein Muster und eine Maßstäblichkeit geschaffen wurden, die zu dem alten Gebäude in Kontrast stehen, aber dennoch analog dazu sind.

Das Raumprogramm für den Anbau forderte eine 930 m² große Kunstbibliothek, eine Galerie für zeitgenössische Kunst, einen Arbeitsbereich für die konservatorische Abteilung, Ateliers für Bildhauerei, Geschäfte und Lernbereiche. Das Projekt beinhaltete außerdem die Renovierung des bestehenden Gebäudes, speziell seiner technischen Einrichtungen. Es war notwendig, ein neues System zur Überprüfung des Raumklimas einzubauen.

Renovation of Allen Memorial Art Museum, Oberlin College, Ohio, 1973

Robert Venturi, John Rauch
Architect in Charge: Jeffery Ryan
Collaborators: Tony Atkin, Janet Colesberry, Stanford Hughes, Dick Rice, Denise Scott Brown
Photography: Collin Tom Bernard

This project was a large extension to a distinguished building designed by Cass Gilbert. To fit the confines of its narrow, constricted site, the addition was placed asymmetrically to the existing building. Particular attention was given to making the addition harmonize with Gilbert's symmetrical Renaissance pavilion. This was accomplished not through imitation but through the careful matching of materials —buff colored brick, red sandstone and pink granite, which were used to produce a pattern and scale in contrast with yet analogous to the old building.

Program requirements for the addition included a 10,000 sq. ft. fine arts library, contemporary art gallery, conservation lab, sculpture studios, shops and study areas. This project also involved renovating the existing building, especially its mechanical systems, which required the introduction of new environmental systems into a masonry building that had no prior humidity control or cooling system.

1. Entwurfsskizze
2. Grundriß erstes Obergeschoß
3. Grundriß Erdgeschoß

1. Preliminary sketch
2. Second floor plan
3. First floor plan

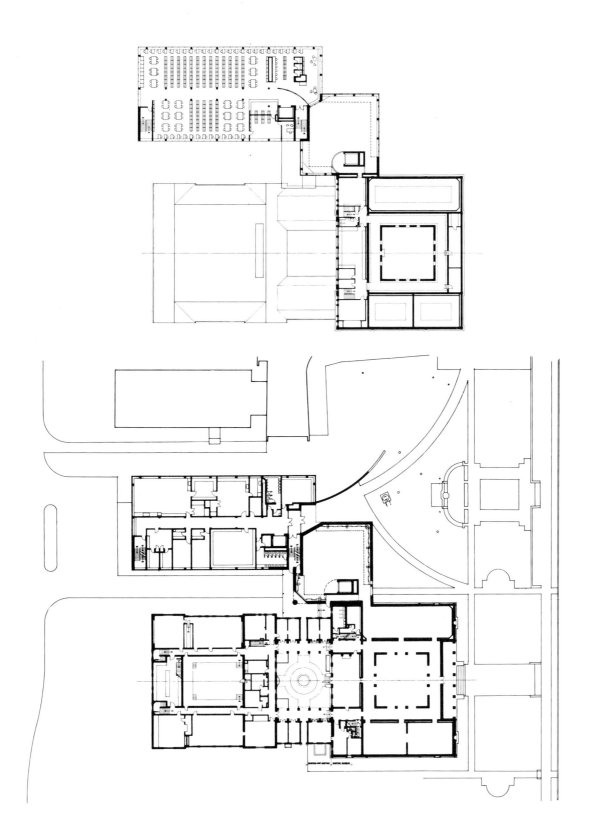

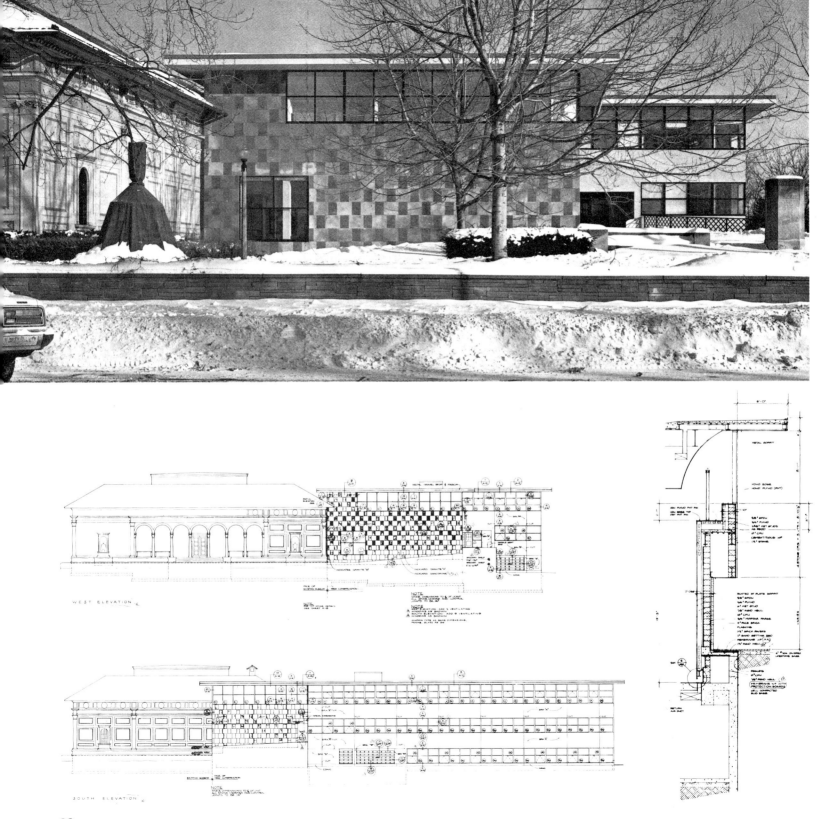

4. Außenansicht der beiden Gebäude
5. West- und Südansicht
6. Ausführungsdetail der Außenwand
7. Rückansicht der Verbindung der beiden Gebäude

4. Exterior view of the two buildings
5. West and South elevations
6. Working detail of the outer wall
7. Back view of the connection of the two buildings

8. Innenansicht
9. Teilansicht der beiden Fassaden
8. Interior view
9. Fragment of the two façades

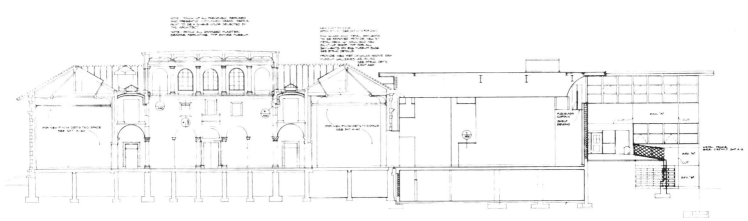

10. Gesamtansicht der seitlichen Fassaden
11. Längsschnitt durch das bestehende Gebäude
12. Eingang des neuen Gebäudes
13. Querschnitt durch das neue Gebäude

10. General view of the side façade
11. Lengthwise section through the existing building
12. Exterior view of the entrance to the new building
13. Cross section through the new building

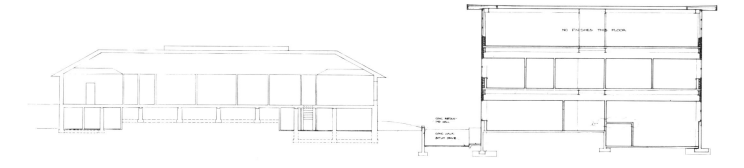

Tuckers Town Haus, Bermuda, 1976
Robert Venturi
Mitwirkender Architekt: John Chase
Fotos: Tom Bernard

Dieses Sommer-Ferienhaus sitzt auf einer zum Meer hin abfallenden Klippe. Der Entwurf entspricht den örtlichen Richtlinien, die einen traditionellen Stil und ebensolche Materialien verlangen. Das Haus besteht aus drei aneinanderhängenden Pavillons: Nebenräume und Küche; Suite der Hausherren, Eßzimmer und andere Schlafzimmer; ein Wohnraum. Die geringe Breite dieser Pavillons ermöglicht eine gute Querlüftung, was in diesem tropischen Klima äußerst wichtig für das Wohlbefinden ist. Die ziegelgedeckten Giebeldächer fangen das Regenwasser auf, eine örtlich gegebene Notwendigkeit. Der Blick zum Meer ist ausgesprochen reizvoll, wenn man das Haus betritt und von der Haupttreppe aus auf den Strand und die dahinterliegende Bucht hinunterschaut.

1. Erd- und Obergeschosse
2. Innenansicht
3. u. 4. Gesamtansichten

Tuckers Town House, Bermuda, 1976
Robert Venturi
Collaborator Architect: John Chase
Photography: Tom Bernard

This summer vacation house is sited on a cliff dropping to a beach. Its design responds to local guidelines requiring use of traditional styles and materials. The house is divided into three abutting pavilions: service areas and kitchen; master suite, dining room, and other sleeping rooms; a living room. The narrowness of these pavilions allows for good cross ventilation, which is crucial for comfort in this tropical climate. The gabled tile roofs are used to collect rainwater, a local necessity. The sea view is dramatically exaggerated on entering the house by the view down the main stair to the beach and the bay beyond.

1. Ground and second floors
2. Interior view
3 and 4. General views

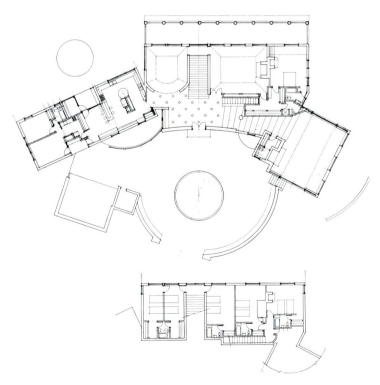

Institute for Scientific Information, Corporate Headquarters, Philadelphia, Pennsylvania, 1978

Robert Venturi, John Rauch
Project Director: David Vaughan
Architects in Charge: Stanford Hughes, Missy Maxwell, Jeffery D. Ryan, James H. Timberlake, Amy Weinstein
Photography: Tom Bernard

The building is a new corporate headquarters for an international scientific information services corporation that uses advanced computer technology. Located in an inner city research park, the site fronts on a major thoroughfare. The client desired «a building that everyone would recognize as a lively and distinctive contribution to the community and to the information industry».

The client's already carefully established program mandated a flat, square building; thin, strip windows; and the location of core elements along one side of the building for future expansion. In addition, the building had to meet the exterior design requirements of the research park; the exterior design requerimentes of the research park; the project schedule for design and construction was highly abbreviated; and the construction budget was quite constrained.

Our design distinguishes the building from its surroundings by imposing on the façade a geometric pattern of colored brick and porcelain panels. The tight, rigorously coded pattern of the overall façade is relieved by the juxtaposition of large abstracted flowers forms marking the main entrance to the building. The freshness of the solution and its contribution to its street brought to one critic's mind the young Louis Sullivan's description of a house by Frank Furness, as «a flower by the side of the road».

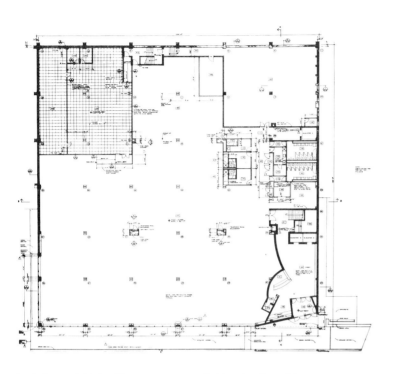

1. Außenansicht des Eingangs
2. Grundriß Erdgeschoß
3. Blick auf die Hauptfassade
4. Hauptansicht

1. Exterior view of the access
2. Ground floor plan
3. General view of the main façade
4. Main elevation

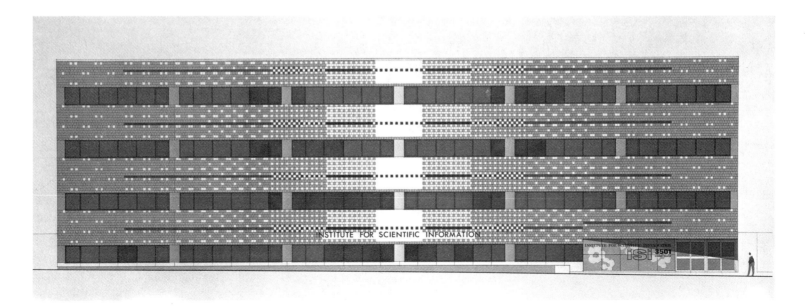

Dixwell Feuerwache, New Haven, Connecticut, 1967
Robert Venturi, John Rauch
Verantwortlicher Architekt: Arthur Jones
Mitarbeiter: Leslie DeLong, Steven Izenour, Robert Renfro, David Vaughan
Fotos: Steven Izenour

Dieses Gebäude, an einer Ecke im Randbereich der Innenstadt von New Haven gelegen, ist großzügig in seinem Maßstab, aber schlicht in seiner Form – es birgt große Elemente in einer einfachen, massigen Form. Das Programm verlangte die üblichen Einrichtungen einer Feuerwache, einschließlich eines Geräteraums für sechs Löschzüge, Nebenräume und Aufenthaltsbereiche für die Feuerwehrmänner. Das Gebäude sitzt diagonal auf dem Grundstück; das ermöglicht ein bestmögliches Ausrücken der Löschfahrzeuge, und die Aufenthaltsbereiche sind dadurch zur Südseite hin ausgerichtet.

Die Beschriftung der Fassade bezeichnet das Gebäude in der für öffentliche Bauten üblichen Weise, aber wo die Buchstaben an die Ecke stoßen, löst sich die Wand ab und kragt aus, um so eine Art Schrifttafel aus Stein zu bilden. Die Ecke des Gebäudes ist abgerundet, um seine diagonale Lage zu mildern und die beiden Straßenfassaden zusammenzuziehen. Das polychrome Ziegelmuster auf der Vorderfront dient dazu, die optische Wirkung der Fassade zu bereichern und den quasi-bürgerlichen Charakter des Gebäudes zu verstärken. Gleichzeitig verleiht der Wechsel von Farben und Details dem niedrigen Gebäude die übliche Aufteilung in Sockelbereich, Mittelteil und oberen Abschluß.

Dixwell Fire Station, New Haven, Connecticut, 1967
Robert Venturi, John Rauch
Architect in Charge: Arthur Jones
Collaborators: Leslie DeLong, Steven Izenour, Robert Renfro, David Vaughan
Photography: Steven Izenour

This building, on a corner at the edge of downtown New Haven, is big in scale but simple in form — it contains big elements in a simple bulk. The program required conventional facilities for a fire station, including a six-truck apparatus room, auxiliary spaces, and living quarters for firemen. The building is located diagonally on the site to permit efficient agress by the trucks and to have the living quarters face south.

The letters on the façade identify it in the traditional manner of civic buildings, but when the letters reach the corner, the wall breaks away and cantilevers to make a kind of brick signboard. The corner of the building is rounded to soften its diagonal placement and to tie the two street façades together. The polychromatic brick pattern on the front is there to enrich the façade and enhance its quasi-civic scale. At the same time, changes in color and detailing give the low building the traditional bottom, mid-level and top.

1. Lageplan, Ansichten und Schnitt
2. Außenansicht des Gebäudes
3. Innenansicht

1. Site plan, elevations and section
2. Exterior view of the building
3. Interior view

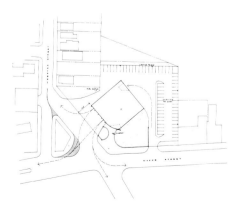
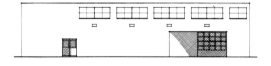
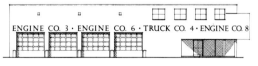

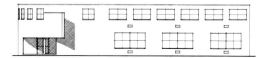

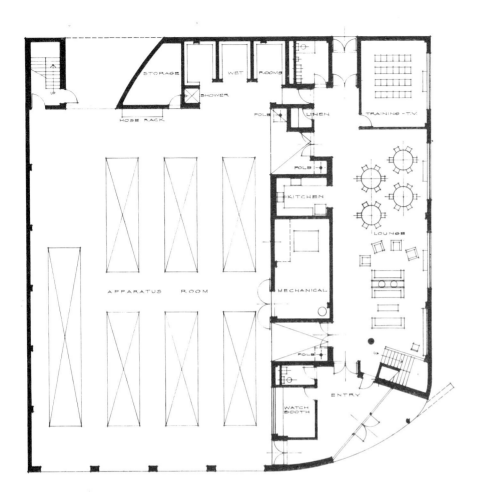

4. Erdgeschoß
5. Ansicht der Seitenfassade
6. Fassadenausschnitt mit Eingang

4. Ground floor
5. Exterior view of the side façade
6. Fragment of the façade with the access

Haus in New Castle, Delaware, 1978

Robert Venturi
Verantwortlicher Architekt: John Chase
Mitarbeiter: Jent Calesberry, Ronald McCoy, Paul Muller, Frederic Schwartz

Dieses Haus für eine dreiköpfige Familie hat ein ungewöhnliches Raumprogramm. Die Ehefrau, eine Musikerin, benötigte ein Musikzimmer für eine Orgel, zwei Klaviere und ein Spinett, das sich außerdem für kleinere Zusammenkünfte eignen sollte. Der Ehemann brauchte einen Arbeitsbereich in einem abgelegenen Teil des Hauses, und auch für den Sohn war eine Reihe von Zimmern verlangt.

Der Grundriß orientiert sich an einer Mittelachse. Die Bibliothek und die Halle, in der der Eßtisch steht, liegen im Erdgeschoß auf einer Achse mit dem Hauptwohnraum, der den Mittelpunkt des Hauses bildet. Das Musikzimmer im ersten Obergeschoß beherrscht den Grundriß. Die großen Fenster dieses Raums sind nach innen zurückgesetzt, um so die Aufheizung durch die Sonne zu verringern. Es ist ein hoher Raum mit einem durchbrochenen Gratgewölbe, den Proportionen der Zimmermanns-Gotik nachempfunden.

Außerdem kennzeichnet das Innere des Hauses eine flache, silhouettenhafte Holzschnitzerei, der die für diese Gegend typischen klassischen Ornamente des 18. und 19. Jahrhunderts als Vorbild diente.

House in New Castle, Delaware, 1978

Robert Venturi
Architect in Charge: John Chase
Collaborators: Janet Colesberry, Ronald McCoy, Paul Muller, Frederic Schwartz

This house for a family of three has an unusual program. The musician wife is a performer who required a music room containing an organ, two pianos, and a hapsichord that must also be appropriate for small gatherings. Birdwatching is another interest of the family so the big windows facing the woods in the breakfast area were important. The husband needed a study in a remote part of the house and a suite of rooms was required for the son.

The house sits in rolling fields at the western edge of a valley with woods to the north. Its form and symbolism is based on the area's traditional 18th century Classical barns which have generous scale and low horizontal proportions — almost Palladian in character, with low porches set into the bulk of the building with stout columns, pent-eaves, and squat openings giving a horizontal emphasis.

The plan is organized around a central axis. The library and the hall, which contains the dining table, are on axis on the ground floor with the main living room dominating the center. Although the music room dominates the plan on the second floor, it is usually closed off to maintain temperature and humidity control for the sake of the musical instruments there. Its big windows are set back to diminish the sun-load. This room is a high space with a latticed groin vault with Carpenter-Gothic proportions. Another feature of the interior of the house is flat, silhouetted ornamentation in wood, based on the area's Classical ornament of the 18th and 19th centuries.

1. Lageplan
2. Grundriß Erdgeschoß
3. Außenansicht mit der Eingangspergola
4. Innenansicht des Musikzimmers
5. Gesamtansicht von außen
6. Innenansicht des Wohn-Eßraums

1. Site plan
2. Ground floor plan
3. Exterior view with the access pergola
4. Interior view of the music room
5. General exterior view
6. Interior view of the living-dining room

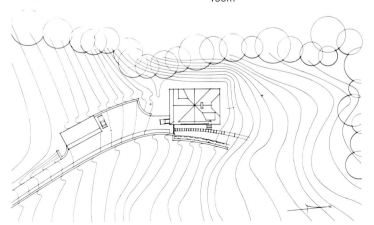
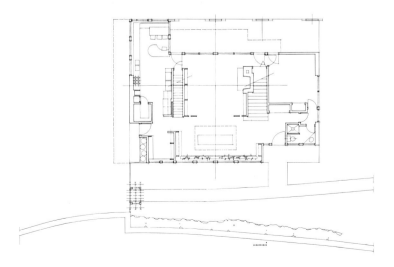

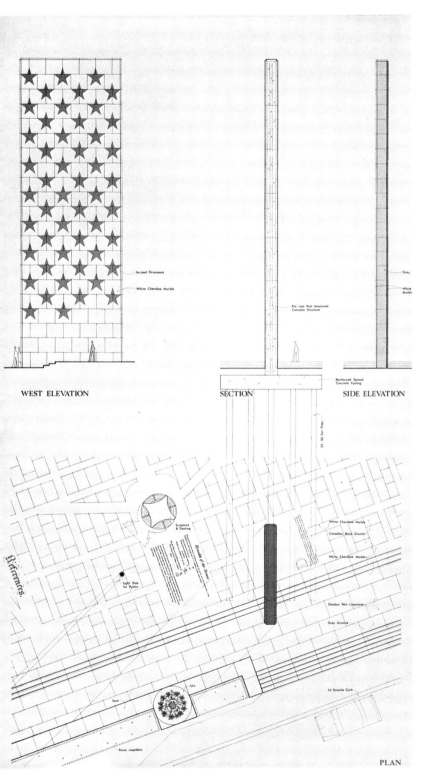

Western Plaza, Pennsylvania Avenue, Washington, D.C., 1977

Robert Venturi, John Rauch
Projektleiter: Jeffrey D. Ryan
Mitarbeiter: Janet Colesberry, Steven Izenour, Stephen Kieran, David Marohn, Missy Maxwell, Frederic Schwartz, Denise Scott Brown, James H. Timberlake

Dieser große städtische Platz bildet den westlichen Abschluß der Pennsylvania Avenue am Weißen Haus und ist umgeben von Büro- und Geschäftshäusern sowie Erholungseinrichtungen. Während der Western Plaza, als Ganzes wahrgenommen, groß und monumental ist, empfindet der Besucher ihn durch die unterschiedlichen gerahmten Blickausschnitte und durch die stufig angelegte Oberfläche als kleiner. Die oberste Terrasse ist über das Straßenniveau angehoben, um so ein Gefühl der Loslösung von den Straßen zu schaffen und um, von den Gehsteigen aus gesehen, dem Platz eine Kante zu geben. Die Einfassung durch Büsche verleiht dem Platz eine weiche Note. Niedrige Mauern dienen als Sitzgelegenheiten.

1. Vorentwurf des Grundrisses und Detail der Säulen
2. Gesamtansicht des Modells
3. Gesamtplan

1. Preliminary design of the plan and detail of the bollards
2. General view of the model
3. General plan

Western Plaza, Pennsylvania Avenue, Washington, D.C., 1977

Robert Venturi, John Rauch
Project Director: Jeffrey D. Ryan
Collaborators: Janet Colesberry, Steven Izenour, Stephen Kieran, David Marohn, Missy Maxwell, Frederic Schwartz, Denise Scott Brown, James H. Timberlake

This large urban plaza terminates the western end of Pennsylvania Avenue at the White House and is adjacent to office, retail, and recreational facilities. While Western Plaza is large and monumental when comprehended as a whole, the visitor perceives it at a smaller scale through a series of framed views and spaces on several terraces. The top terrace is elevated above street level to create a sense of separation from the streets and to create and edge to the piazza seen from the sidewalks. An edging of shrubbery adds a touch of softness. Low walls act as seats.

The design resolves the disrupted axial relationship between the White House and the Capitol and develops a monumental scale and powerful focus appropriate to its location.

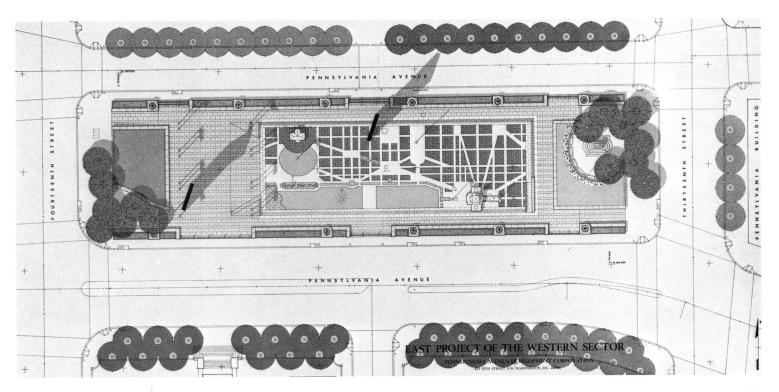

4. Detail der Gegend um den Platz mit dem Reiterstandbild
5. Perspektivischer Blick auf das Weiße Haus auf dem Platz und das echte im Hintergrund
6. Platz aus der Vogelperspektive

4. Detail of the area of the plaza with the equestrian statue
5. Perspective view of the White House, in the plaza and in reality in the background
6. Bird's eye view of the plaza

Ausstellungshalle für Produkte der Firma Best, Oxford Valley, Pennsylvania, 1977
Robert Venturi, John Rauch
Mitarbeiter: Stanford Hughes, Virginia Jacobs, Robert Renfro, Denise Scott Brown
Fotos: Tom Bernard, Steven Izenour

Best Products Catalog Showroom, Oxford Valley, Pennsylvania, 1977
Robert Venturi, John Rauch
Architect in Charge: David Vaughan
Collaborators: Stanford Hughes, Virginia Jacobs, Robert Renfro, Denise Scott Brown
Photography: Tom Bernard, Steven Izenour

Diese Ausstellungshalle liegt inmitten riesiger Parkflächen und zahlreicher sich kreuzender Straßen um ein großes Einkaufszentrum. Das serienmäßig hergestellte Standardgebäude ohne Fenster bedurfte eines Designs auf der Außenhaut, um es an seinem diffizilen Standort hervorzuheben.

Freistehend auf einem Parkplatz errichteten wir das Gebäude aus einer elementierten Stahlrahmenkonstruktion mit Ausfachungen und entwickelten eine dekorative Fassade aus porzellan-emaillierten Paneelen. Große abstrakte rote und weiße Blumen wurden wegen ihrer starken Anziehungskraft auf den Betrachter aufgetragen, während der willkürliche »Tapeteneffekt« des über die Paneelflächen und über die Kanten des Gebäudes hinauslaufenden Musters die zweidimensionale grafische Wirkung verstärkte. Es wurde eine Standardisierung gewählt, um die Anzahl der Arbeitsschritte bei der Herstellung der Paneele zu minimieren. Die großen »Signale« auf diesem niedrigen Gebäude sind bei diesem ungewöhnlichen Projekt äußerst wirkungsvoll.

This catalog showroom is located in an area of vast parking lots and numerous crossroads surrounding a major shopping mall. It needed a desing for the exterior of a standard mass produced building with no windows that would give it a noticeable presence and recognition in its difficult location.

Working within the parameters of a steel frame structure with block infill, freestanding in a parking lot, we developed a decorative façade fabricated out of porcelain steel panels. Large abstract red and white flowers were chosen for their obvious appeal to the viewer, while the random «wallpaper» effect of the overall pattern in relation to the panel module and the edges of the building reinforced to two-dimensional graphic scale of the pattern. A standard repeat was used to minimize the screens in fabricating the panels. The big «sign» on the low building are combined to great effect in this unusual project.

1. Detail der Blumenkomposition auf den Paneelen
2. Fassadenausschnitt

1. Details of the floral compositions in the panels
2. Fragment of the façade

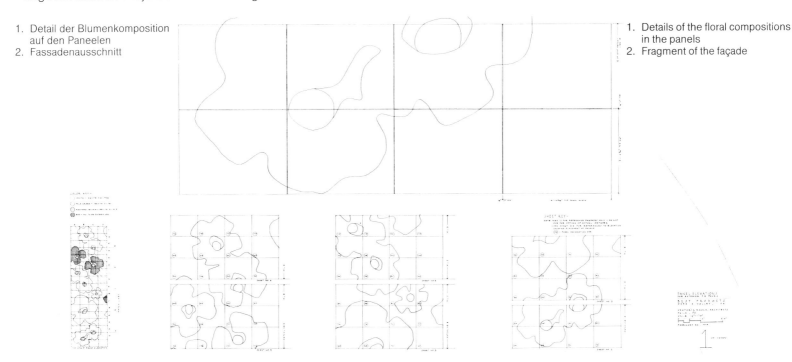

3. Außenansicht der Fassade
4. Detail des Blumenmusters

3. Exterior view of the main façade
4. Detail of the floral composition

Museum für Kunsthandwerk, Wettbewerb, Frankfurt, Bundesrepublik Deutschland, 1979

Robert Venturi
Projektleiter: David Vaughan
Mitarbeiter: James Bradberry, Lee Rayburn, Frederic Schwartz, Denise Scott Brown, James H. Timberlake

In dem Entwurf für dieses zirka 11150 m² große Museumsgebäude waren auch eine bestehende Villa aus dem 19. Jahrhundert und ein angrenzender 120 Ar großer Park am Südufer des Main einzubeziehen. Es wurde versucht, den Wohngebietscharakter der historischen Straße beizubehalten, und zwar indem der Maßstab und der Rhythmus der bestehenden Fenster wiederholt und die Höhe des Gebäudes an der Straße denen der benachbarten Stadthäuser angeglichen wurde. Der Park sollte als Ausstellungsfläche für historische Funde dienen.

1. Gesamtansicht des Modells
2. Grundriß Erdgeschoß
3. Grundriß erstes Obergeschoß
4. Grundriß drittes Obergeschoß
5. Ausschnitt aus dem Innenraum
6. Detailschnitt durch die Wände der Nord- und Südfassade
7. Ansicht der Hauptfassade

Museum fur Kunsthandwerk (Decorative Arts) Competition, Frankfurt, West Germany, 1979

Robert Venturi
Project Director: David Vaughan
Collaborators: James Bradberry, Lee Rayburn, Frederic Schwartz, Denise Scott Brown, James H. Timberlake

The design for this museum building of approximately 120,000 square feet, also incorporated an existing 19th century villa, and an adjacent four-acre park, on the south bank of the Main River. The design of the addition sought to respect the residential character of the historic street by repeating the scale and rhythm of the existing windows and by limiting the height at the street to that of the townhouses nearby. The park was designed to accomodate the historic relics to be located there.

1. General view of the model
2. Ground floor plan
3. Second floor plan
4. Fourth floor plan
5. Detail of the interior
6. Working details of the North and South façades' walls
7. Elevation of the main façade

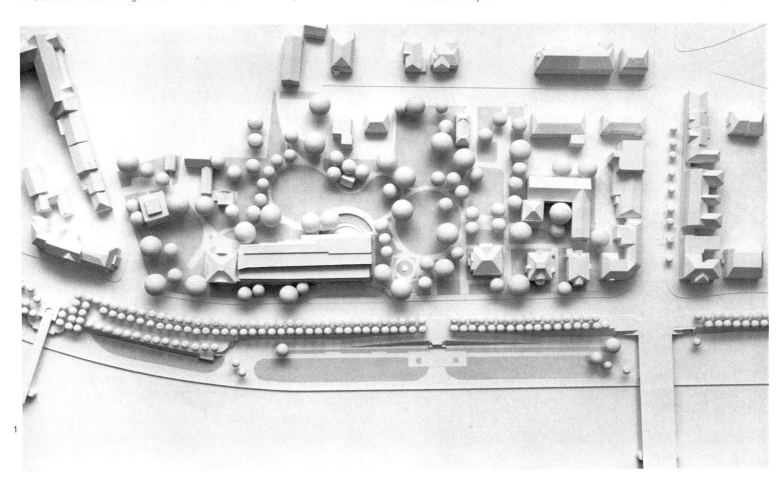

1

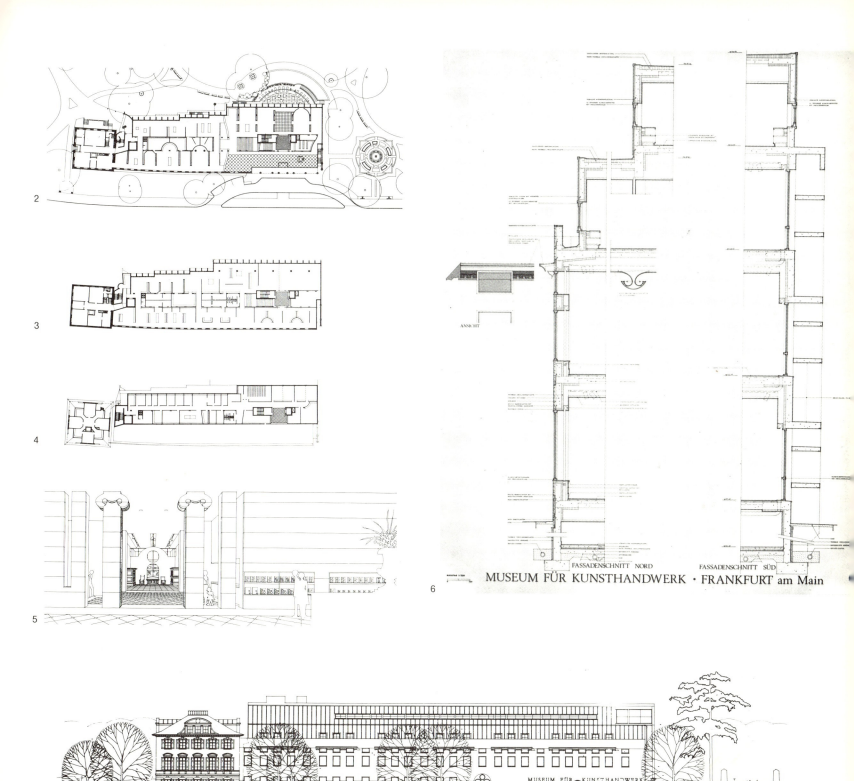

Haus in Vail, Colorado, 1975
Robert Venturi
Verantwortlicher Architekt: Robert Renfro
Mitarbeiter: Elisabeth Plater-Zyberk, Doug Southworth
Fotos: Steven Izenour

Dieses Haus steht, umgeben von Espen und niedrigen immergrünen Büschen, an einem steilen Nordhang des Gebirges oberhalb von Vail. Entworfen wurde es für eine junge Familie mit zwei Kindern und einem Freund, es sollte aber auch Platz für zahlreiche Gäste bieten.

Es wurde ein viergeschossiger Turm zwischen die hohen, geraden Bäume gestellt. Im ersten Geschoß sind Lagerraum, Waschküche und Sauna untergebracht, im zweiten Schlafzimmer und kleine Zimmer mit eingebauten Betten für die Gäste. Das dritte beherbergt Küche, Eßplätze und einen separaten Raum, der als Fernseh- und Spielzimmer für die Kinder oder als Gästezimmer genutzt werden kann. Das vierte Geschoß, das zwischen den Baumwipfeln liegt, hat große Mansardenfenster mit tiefen Fensterbänken, die man als Betten für zusätzliche Gäste nutzen kann. Der Fußboden ist aus breiten Kieferbrettern, die Wandvertäfelung innen und außen aus Zedernholz. Möbliert ist das Haus überwiegend mit Eichenmöbeln im Gustav Stickley Mission-Style.

House in Vail, Colorado, 1975
Robert Venturi
Architect in Charge: Robert Renfro
Collaborators: Elisabeth Plater-Zyberk, Doug Southworth
Photography: Steven Izenour

This ski is on the steep northern slope of the mountain above Vail in a beautiful stand of aspen trees and low evergreen bushes. It was designed for a young family with two children and a friend and also to accommodate a large number of guests.

The building is a four-story tower at home among the tall, straight trees. The first story contains storage, laundry, and sauna facilities. The second contains bedrooms and small bunkrooms to accommodate guests. The third contains the kitchen and dining spaces with a separate room to be used as playroom-TV room for the children and as a guest room. The fourth floor is in the tree tops with big dormer windows containing window seats that can also be used as beds for additional guests. The flooring is wide pine planks; there is cedar siding inside and out and it is furnished mostly with a collection of Gustav Stickley Mission oak furniture.

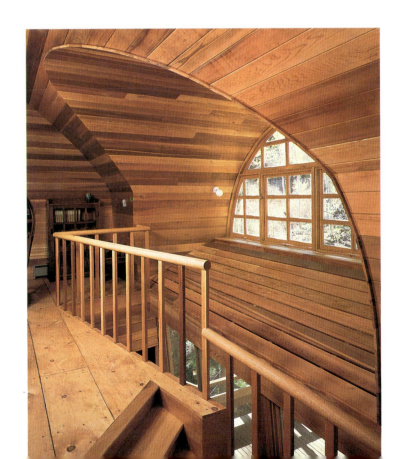

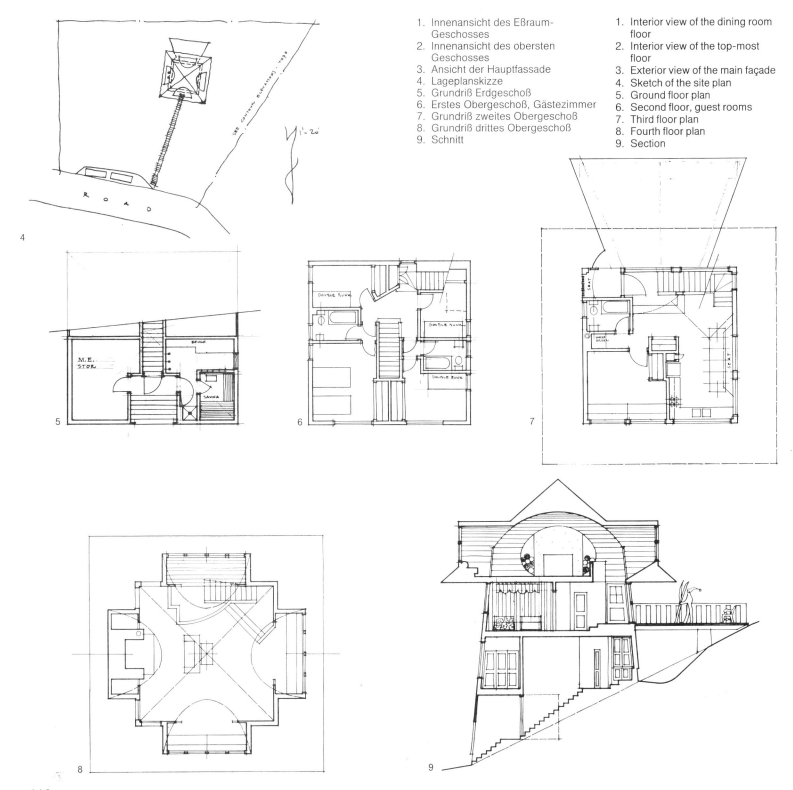

1. Innenansicht des Eßraum-Geschosses
2. Innenansicht des obersten Geschosses
3. Ansicht der Hauptfassade
4. Lageplanskizze
5. Grundriß Erdgeschoß
6. Erstes Obergeschoß, Gästezimmer
7. Grundriß zweites Obergeschoß
8. Grundriß drittes Obergeschoß
9. Schnitt

1. Interior view of the dining room floor
2. Interior view of the top-most floor
3. Exterior view of the main façade
4. Sketch of the site plan
5. Ground floor plan
6. Second floor, guest rooms
7. Third floor plan
8. Fourth floor plan
9. Section

10. Detail der Sitzbank
11. Detail des Vorbaus am Eingang
12. Innenansicht

10. Detail of the bench
11. Detail of the access porch
12. Interior view

Hennepin Avenue, Minneapolis, Minnesota, 1981
Denise Scott Brown mit Benne-Ringrose-Wolsfeld-Jarvis-Gardner Inc.
Verantwortlicher Architekt: James H. Timberlake

In Phase I dieses Projekts ging es um den Entwurf einer Verkehrsstraße durch ein sieben Blocks umfassendes Vergnügungsviertel. Wegen seiner Nähe zu einem zentralen Geschäfts- und Bankenviertel planten wir, dem Boulevard ein bei Tag und Nacht einzigartig und festlich wirkendes Image zu verleihen. Neue dekorative Beleuchtungskörper, überdachte Haltestellen, Plätze, Straßenmöblierung und Bepflasterung waren die Schlüsselelemente in diesem Entwurf. Empfehlungen für den Entwurf angrenzender Strukturen, ihre Anwendung und Richtlinien für die über Straßenniveau liegenden Fußgängerüberführungen waren ebenso in der Phase I enthalten.

Hennepin Avenue Transit, Minneapolis, Minnesota, 1981
Denise Scott Brown, with the Bennet-Ringrose-Wolsfeld-Jarvis-Gardner Inc.
Architect in Charge: James H. Timberlake

Phase I of this project included the design of new transit facilities in an entertainment district seven blocks long. The Avenue, owing to its proximity to the central retail and banking district of Minneapolis, was designed to have a unique, festive image at day and night. New decorative lights, enclosed transit shelters, outdoor plazas, street furniture and paving are the key elements in the design. Recommendations for the design of adjacent structures, their uses and guidelines for the skyways crossing streets were also included within the Phase I design package.

1. Perspektive
2. Ansicht bei Nacht

1. Perspective
2. Night view

Gordon Wu Hall, Butler College, Princeton, New Jersey, 1980
Robert Venturi, John Rauch
Mitarbeiter: Arthur Jones, Missy Maxwell, David Marohn, James Timberlake, Stan Runijan, Ronald G. McCoy

Gordon Wu Hall ist der neue Mittelpunkt des Butler College, eines der drei neuen Wohn-Colleges von Princeton, und beherbergt Speisesaal, Gesellschaftsraum, Bibliothek, Lernbereiche und Büros für die Verwaltung. Schwierig an dem Entwurf war, auf einem ungleichmäßigen, geneigten und schmalen Grundstück ein Gebäude unterzubringen, das dem neuen College Identität verleihen, als Mittelpunkt seines sozialen Lebens dienen und seine Anbindung an andere Einrichtungen des Butler College in zwei bereits existierenden Gebäuden ungleichen Stils verdeutlichen sollte.

Der lange Speisesaal erhält durch das hohe Ausluchtfenster an seinem Ende Größe und Würde – er erinnert an die neu-gotischen Speisesäle von Princeton –, aber niedrige Decken, große Fenster und die Möblierung aus Naturholz geben dem Raum einen intimen und gemütlichen Charakter und machen aus ihm eine angenehme Mischung aus Café und feierlichem Speisesaal. Von der Eingangshalle aus führt eine Treppe an einem weiteren Ausluchtfenster vorbei zum Gesellschaftsraum, den Büros der Verwaltung und der Bibliothek im Obergeschoß. Der erste Treppenlauf weitet sich auf der einen Seite überraschend zu tribünenartigen Sitzstufen aus. Der erweiterte Treppenraum suggeriert eine feierliche, in

Gordon Wu Hall, Butler College, Princeton, New Jersey, 1980
Robert Ventury, John Rauch
Collaborators: Arthur Jones, Missy Maxwell, David Mahron, James Timberlake, Stan Runijan, Ronald G. McCoy

Gordon Wu Hall provides a new focus for Butler College, one of Princeton's three new residential colleges, and houses its dining hall, lounge, library, study areas, and administrative offices. The design problem was to create a building on an irregular, sloping and narrow site that would provide an identity for the new college, serve as a focal point for its social life and give a sense of cohesiveness with other Butler Colleges facilities in two already existing buildings of disparate styles. A further requirement was that Wu Hall share an existing kitchen with adjacent Wilson College.

The interior of the building was planned not only to create a series of spaces to accommodate the social and dining activities of 500 students, but also to provide opportunities for informal, intimate and spontaneous social interaction. The long dining room with a tall bay window at its end provides a sense of grandeur and recalls Princeton's neo-Gothic dining halls, but low ceilings, large windows and natural wood furnishings create another scale of intimacy and comfort that allows the large room to become a pleasing cross between a cafe and a grand dining commons. At the entry lobby a stairway leads past another large bay window to a lounge administrative offices and library on the upper floor. The first flight of stairs unex-

1. Schrägansicht
2. Ansicht Hauptfassade
3. Grundriß erstes Obergeschoß
4. Grundriß Erdgeschoß

1. Slanted general view
2. Elevation main façade
3. Second floor plan
4. First floor plan

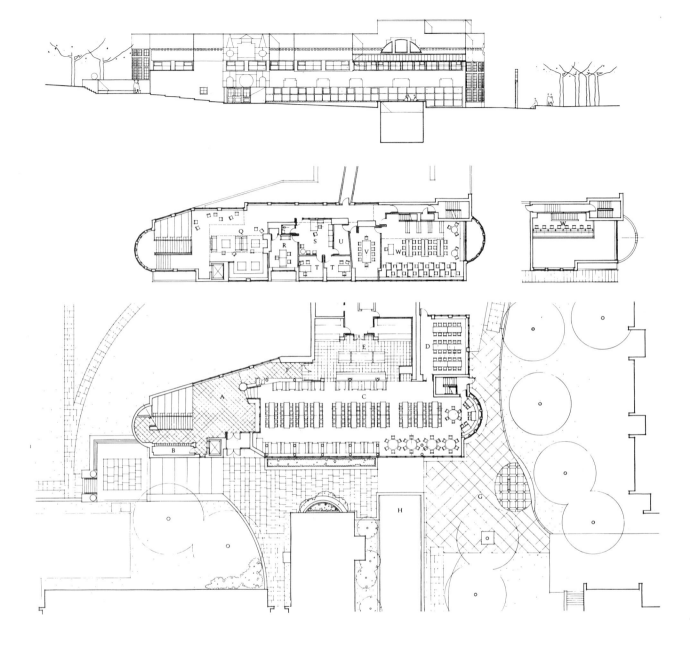

weitem Bogen nach oben führende Treppe, dient aber zwanglos als spontaner Warte- und Versammlungsort. Bei besonderen Gelegenheiten wird er zum innenliegenden Amphitheater.

Die Außenwände aus rotem Ziegel mit Fenstergewänden aus Kalkstein und die großen Ausluchtfenster an beiden Enden verbinden Wu Hall mit den andern gotischen Gebäuden der Universität. Durch die Art, wie es sich zwischen die anderen Gebäude einfügt, bewirkt das Gebäude eine formale Einheit dieses vorher undefinierten Teils des Campus.

pectedly extends to one side to form bleacher-like risers suitable for sitting. The extended stairwell suggests a grand stair sweeping upward, but serves informally as a spontaneous waiting and gathering place. On special occasions it becomes an indoor amphitheater.

The red brick outerwalls with limestone window trim and the large bay windows at both ends of the building link Wu Hall to the older Gothic buildings of the University Slid as it is between other buildings, it brings form and coherence to a once undefined portion of the Campus.

5. Gesamtansicht
6. Innenansicht des Speisesaals
7. Eingangsdetail

5. General view
6. Interior view of the dining room
7. Detail of the access

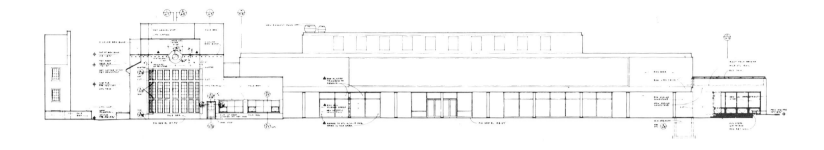

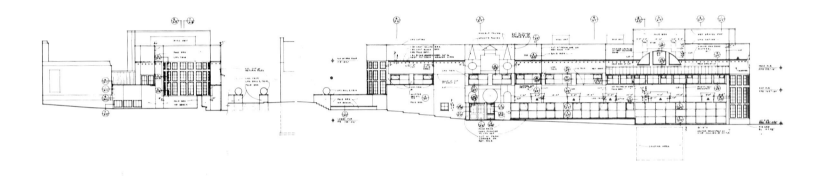

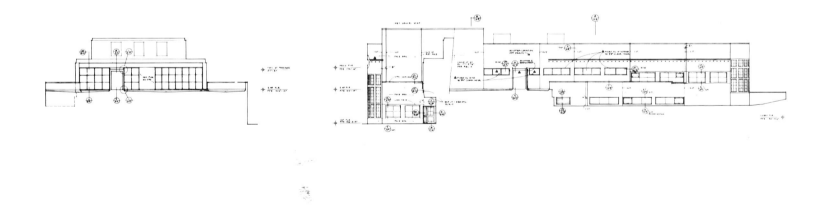

8. Ansicht Südseite
9. Ansichten Nord- und Westseite
10. Ansicht Ostseite
11. Innenansicht der Treppenränge

8. South elevation
9. North and West elevations
10. East elevation
11. Interior view of the stairs-tiers

Gebäude für Molekularbiologie, Princeton University, Princeton, New Jersey, 1983–1985
Robert Venturi
Projektleiter: Ronald McCoy
Mitarbeiter: Margo Angevino, Rick Buckley, Sam Harris, David Shaaf, James H. Timberlake

Das Gebäude für Molekularbiologie ist vorne drei-, hinten viergeschossig, dem nach Süden abfallenden Gelände entsprechend. Die Fassaden des Gebäudes, das heißt Aufteilung, Rhythmus und Proportion, wurden durch besondere Programmvorgaben für die Innenaufteilung bestimmt. Die beiden Längsfassaden bestehen aus einer im wesentlichen gleichmäßigen Aufteilung in identische Felder, entsprechend dem einheitlichen Raumraster – räumlich, konstruktiv und technisch –, wie es sich aus dem Modul von 3,35 m für die Labors herleitet. Diese Felder sind mittels sich wiederholender Fenstergruppen gekennzeichnet, die nach außen hin jeweils einen technischen Bereich widerspiegeln. Die Felder bereichern die Fassade und unterstreichen die strenge Form des Gebäudes. An der Südseite liegen die Fenster weiter zurück, um eine natürliche Verschattung zu erzielen; aus diesem Grund konnte ungetöntes Glas verwendet werden,

Molecular Biology Building, Princeton University, Princeton, New Jersey, 1983-1985
Robert Venturi
Project Director: Ronald McCoy
Collaborators: Margo Angevino, Rick Buckley, Sam Harris, David Shaaf, James H. Timberlake

The Molecular Biology building is three stories in front, four stories in back, reflecting the site's slope to the south. The building's façades, in terms of scale, rhythm, and proportion are determined by particular requirements of program and interior layout. The two long elevations consist of an essentially consistent rhythm of identical bays reflecting the repetitive bays inside —spatial, structural, and mechanical— accommodating the lab-office module of 11 feet. These bays are articulated via repetitive window bays accommodating a mechanical zone on the exterior wall and promoting a surface richness wich complements the severity of the overall form of the building. On the south side the windows are recessed to provide natural sunshading, allowing the use of untinted glass and adding a richer sculptural effect to the façade.

Alternating bands of patterned brick and large windows with cast stone trim wrap the perimeter of the building. A recessive brick and cast stone pattern differentiates the high upper floor, devoted to the mechanical plant. The exterior materials, brick, granite and cast stone trim, also relate to the typical building materials of this area of the campus. Both end elevations depart from the rectangular nature of the building, having large bay windows on each level providing lounges which terminate the two wide interior passageways, improving circulation and relieving the required repetitive laboratory and office spaces opening off the corridors.

The variety and texture of these surfaces create several orders of scale and lend interest to the building's extremely long façade and complement the many orders of scale of the traditional Collegiate Gothic architecture of Guyot Hall complex, the existing Geology and Biology Departments, located to the north across College Walk.

For durability and richness, oak is used on wall rails, doors, furniture and casework. This use of a natural material quietly humanizes the highly technical laboratory environment. These interior arrangements accommodated by the exterior, work to offer a safe, effective workplace, one adaptive to both short and long term change, sensitive to both individual and University needs.

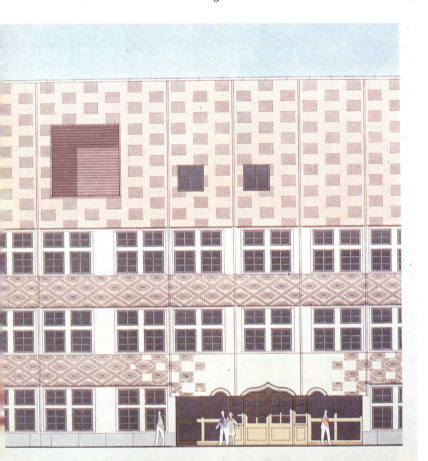

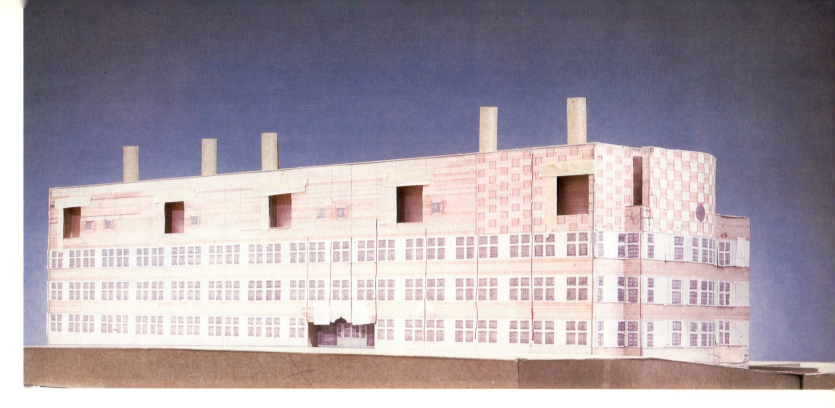

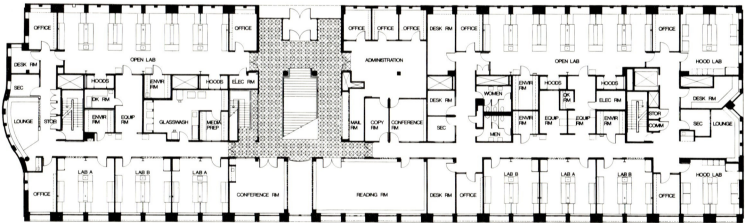

und gleichzeitig wurde die plastische Wirkung der Fassade verstärkt.

Reihen abwechselnder Ziegelmuster und großer Fenster mit Betonsteineinfassungen laufen um das gesamte Gebäude. Ein dezentes Muster aus Ziegel- und Betonstein betont das hohe oberste Stockwerk, in dem sich die technischen Anlagen befinden. Die äußeren Materialien Ziegel, Granit und Betonsteineinfassungen stellen auch einen Bezug her zu den typischen Baumaterialien der Gebäude auf diesem Teil des Campus. Die beiden Schmalseiten des Gebäudes weichen durch große Ausluchtfenster in allen Stockwerken von der rechteckigen Form des Gebäudes ab; dahinter verbergen sich Aufenthaltsräume, die als Endpunkte der beiden breiten Flure den Verkehrsfluß verbessern, indem sie den vorgegebenen Rhythmus der Labor- und Büroräume auflockern und die Korridore erweitern.

1. Ausschnitt aus der Hauptfassade
2. Gesamtansicht des Modells
3. Grundriß Erdgeschoß

1. Portion of the main façade elevation
2. General view of the model
3. First floor plan

than placing the dome over the sanctuary where it would create a central focus within, we have placed it over the sahn. Its use over the exterior space of the sahn, which is used as outdoor space for worship, is particularly suitable. On the inside, the dome reveals itself as a tree within a courtyard, a huge tree, but light and airy, whose great uplifted canopy shades the sahn and the people beneath.

Our principal guiding ideas, then, have been to develop a building in which the scale and elements express monumentality in architecture as well as stress human scale; in which the spatial layout is unequivocally egalitarian; and finally, where symbolic elements such as the arcades, ornament, dome, muqarnas, crenelations, and minaret have clear and acceptable referents. This approach to the design of the State Mosque should generate a majestic image from without and a series of profoundly moving spaces from within.

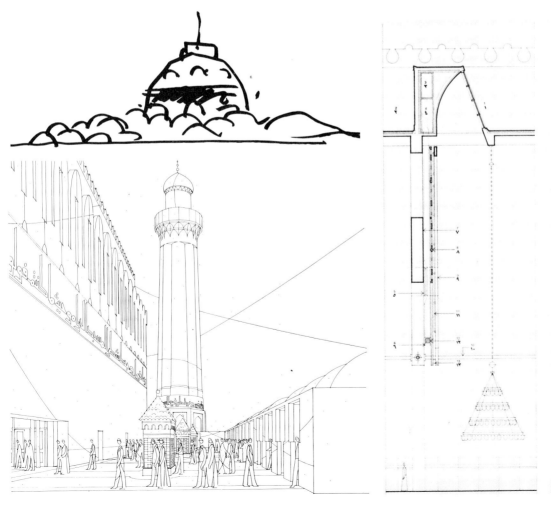

2. Ansicht Nordseite
3. Entwurfsskizze
4. Perspektive
5. Detailschnitt durch die Wand
6. Innendetail des Mihrab und der Bögen
7. Innenperspektive

2. Elevation of the North façade
3. Preliminary sketch
4. Perspective
5. Detailed section of the wall
6. Interior detail of the mirhab and the arches
7. Interior perspective

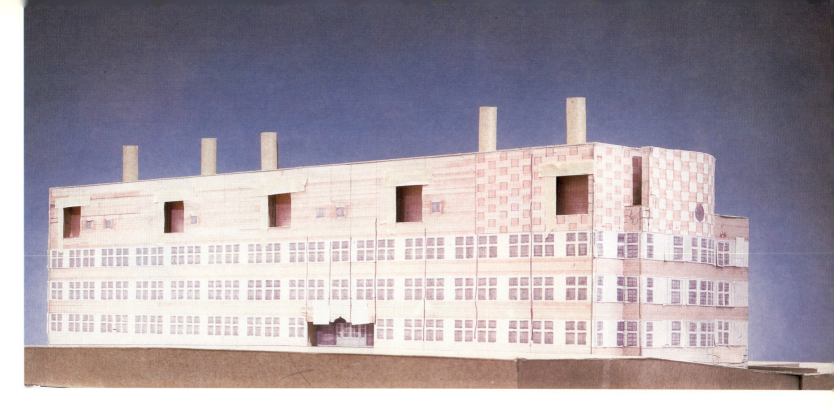

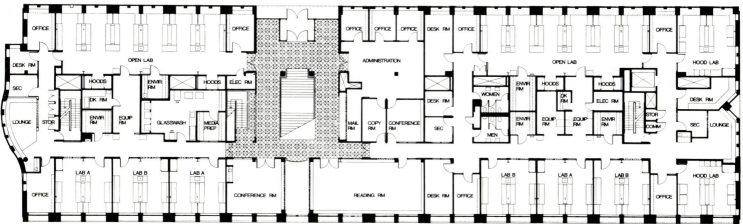

und gleichzeitig wurde die plastische Wirkung der Fassade verstärkt.

Reihen abwechselnder Ziegelmuster und großer Fenster mit Betonsteineinfassungen laufen um das gesamte Gebäude. Ein dezentes Muster aus Ziegel- und Betonstein betont das hohe oberste Stockwerk, in dem sich die technischen Anlagen befinden. Die äußeren Materialien Ziegel, Granit und Betonsteineinfassungen stellen auch einen Bezug her zu den typischen Baumaterialien der Gebäude auf diesem Teil des Campus. Die beiden Schmalseiten des Gebäudes wei-

chen durch große Ausluchtfenster in allen Stockwerken von der rechteckigen Form des Gebäudes ab; dahinter verbergen sich Aufenthaltsräume, die als Endpunkte der beiden breiten Flure den Verkehrsfluß verbessern, indem sie den vorgegebenen Rhythmus der Labor- und Büroräume auflockern und die Korridore erweitern.

1. Ausschnitt aus der Hauptfassade
2. Gesamtansicht des Modells
3. Grundriß Erdgeschoß

1. Portion of the main façade elevation
2. General view of the model
3. First floor plan

Staatsmoschee, Bagdad, Irak, 1983

Robert Venturi
Projektleiter: Steven Izenour, David Marohn
Mitarbeiter: Reyhan Larimar, Rick Buckley, Erica Gees, John Hays, David Hinson, Mike Levin, Bob Marker, Chris Matheu, Dan McCoubrey, Miles Ritter, Lou Rodilico, Simon Tickell, Maurice Weintraub

Eine Staatsmoschee für den Irak zu entwerfen, ist eine Herausforderung. Der Entwurf muß große Probleme konstruktiver und funktioneller Art lösen, die immer dann auftreten, wenn eine große Zahl von Benutzern betroffen ist. Und er muß dabei feinfühlig den städtebaulichen und den unmittelbaren Kontext berücksichtigen sowie den Stellenwert, den Symbolik und Ornamentik im kulturellen und religiösen Erbe des Islam im allgemeinen und in dem des Irak im speziellen einnehmen. Das Image einer Staatsmoschee muß gleichzeitig tiefgründig sein, um zu überdauern, und populär, um von der heutigen Bevölkerung des Irak angenommen zu werden.

Um die Moschee auch von weitem als solche erkennbar zu machen, verwendeten wir traditionelle Elemente wie die Stalaktitenkuppel und das Minarett; die Moschee ist so bei Tag und Nacht von jedem Punkt der Stadt aus sichtbar. Die städtebauliche Anwendung dieser traditionellen Formen ist allgemein verständlich.

Wir haben uns für den Grundriß eines Hypostyls entschieden, um moderne Konstruktionstechniken ausnutzen zu können. Die Arkadenreihen, die die Form des Altarraums definieren, liegen weit über Kopfhöhe und werden von oben her getragen, so daß der große Raum hoch oben von den Arkaden unterteilt wird, während er unten relativ offen bleibt. Für ankommende oder weggehende Gläubige ist der Anblick der sich wiederholenden Arkaden mit ihrem Spiel aus Licht und Dekoration erhebend und majestätisch. Diese Eigenschaften ebnen den Weg für ein bewegendes Erlebnis für den einzelnen oder die Gruppe während der Gebetsstunde. Es herrscht dann ein Gefühl von Einheit und Ruhe vor.

Von außen ist die Kuppel das tragende Symbol der Moschee, ihr leuchtendes, dreidimensionales Aussehen ist aus der Entfernung eine Abrundung für das Stadtbild von Bagdad. Anstatt die Kuppel über den Altarraum zu setzen, der damit zum zentralen Mittelpunkt geworden wäre, haben wir sie über den Sahn plaziert. Als Überdachung des Sahn, der als außenliegender Gebetsraum genutzt wird, ist sie von besonderem Nutzen. Innen wirkt die Kuppel wie der Baum in einem Hof, ein sehr hoher, aber heller und luftiger Baum, da ihr großer erhöhter Baldachin dem Sahn und den Menschen Schatten bringt.

State Mosque, Baghdad, Irak, 1983

Robert Venturi
Project Directors: Steven Izenour, David Morohn
Collaborators: Reyhan Larimar, Rick Buckley, Erica Gees, John Hays, David Hinson, Mike Levin, Bob Marker, Chris Matheu, Dan McCoubrey, Miles Ritter, Lou Rodilico, Simon Tickell, Maurice Weintraub

The challenge of the design for a State Mosque for Iraq is awesome. It must solve formidable problems of structure and function that arise when large numbers of users are involved and it must do so with sensitivity to the urban and environmental context and with a deep understanding of the symbolic and ornamental dimensions thar are embodied in the cultural and religious heritage of Islam in general and of Iraq in particular. The image of a State Mosque must be at once profound, to speak to future ages, and popular, to be loved by the people of Iraq today.

In trying to fulfill these ideals we turned to the hypostyle plan, the primordial mosque space throughout the Islamic world. Particularly important examples of this type, such as the mosque of al-Mutawakkil at Samarra, were native to Iraq and were the prototypes for mosques elsewhere. The simple boxlike form of the hypostyle mosque, by its very nature, does not dominate its surroundings by three-dimensional form or mass. The context of the site, a loose fabric of roads and small scale housing, demands even more strongly that the mosque have important architectural and urban presence.

To identify the mosque at a distance we are employing the traditional elements of a muqarnas dome and minaret to locate the mosque across the city both day and night. This urbanistic use of traditional forms will be understood by all.

To give the mosque scale and symbolism in the middle distance, we have done two things. We have grouped the ancillary facilities of school, library, and residential complex in a cluster at the base of the east wall of the mosque so that as visitors approach along Rabia Street, they see the great wall of the mosque rising above the simple, traditional forms of this «urban quarter» in the foreground. Second, we have carefully controlled the sequence and vista of the vehicular approach. The entry road off of Rabia Street sweeps in a tightening spiral across the north front of the mosque. As visitors drive along, they view the mosque through rows of towering date palms.

Seen through the screen of date palms, the State Mosque sits on a sand-colored court. Its immense wall is crested by a turquoise and white band of inscription and large scale merlons. A vast muqarnas dome seems almost to float above the weightier masonry walls.

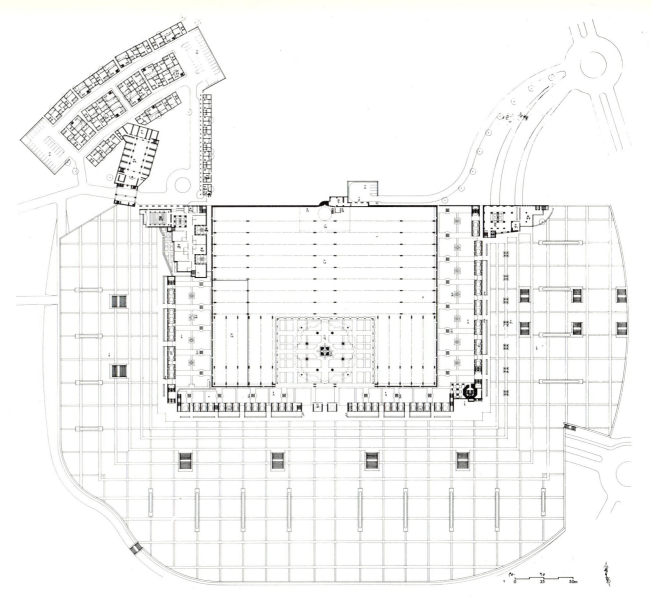

Unsere Leitidee war dann, ein Gebäude zu entwerfen, dessen Maßstab und Elemente Monumentalität in der Architektur ausdrücken, das aber auch den menschlichen Maßstab hervorhebt; ein Gebäude, dessen räumliche Aufteilung eindeutig egalitär ist; ein Gebäude schließlich, dessen symbolische Elemente wie Arkaden, Ornamente, Kuppel, Mukarnas, Zinnenkränze und Minarett einen klaren und verständlichen Bezug haben. Diese Art des Entwurfs soll der Staatsmoschee ein majestätisches Äußeres geben und innen tief beeindruckende Räume schaffen.

We have adapted the hypostyle plan to take advantage of modern construction techniques. The series of arcades which define the form of the sanctuary are lifted high overhead and are supported from above, so that the great space is delineated by the arcades aloft but left relatively open below. To worshippers entering or leaving, the view of the repeated arcades with their play of light and decoration is uplifting and majestic. These qualities prepare the way for a moving experience for the individual or group at the time of prayer. The feeling overall is one of unity and serenity.

The dome is a major symbol of the mosque from outside, where its vivid, three-dimensional image is seen from a distance, complementing the view of the city of Baghdad. Rather

1. Grundriß   1. Ground floor

than placing the dome over the sanctuary where it would create a central focus within, we have placed it over the sahn. Its use over the exterior space of the sahn, which is used as outdoor space for worship, is particularly suitable. On the inside, the dome reveals itself as a tree within a courtyard, a huge tree, but light and airy, whose great uplifted canopy shades the sahn and the people beneath.

Our principal guiding ideas, then, have been to develop a building in which the scale and elements express monumentality in architecture as well as stress human scale; in which the spatial layout is unequivocally egalitarian; and finally, where symbolic elements such as the arcades, ornament, dome, muqarnas, crenelations, and minaret have clear and acceptable referents. This approach to the design of the State Mosque should generate a majestic image from without and a series of profoundly moving spaces from within.

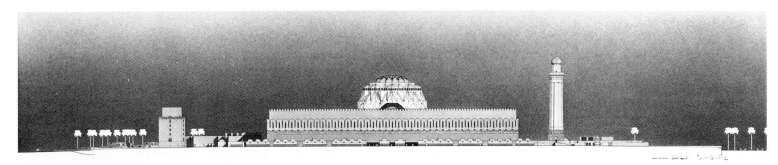

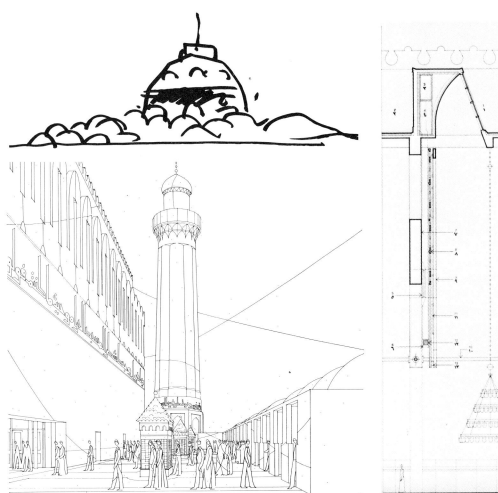

2. Ansicht Nordseite
3. Entwurfsskizze
4. Perspektive
5. Detailschnitt durch die Wand
6. Innendetail des Mihrab und der Bögen
7. Innenperspektive

2. Elevation of the North façade
3. Preliminary sketch
4. Perspective
5. Detailed section of the wall
6. Interior detail of the mirhab and the arches
7. Interior perspective

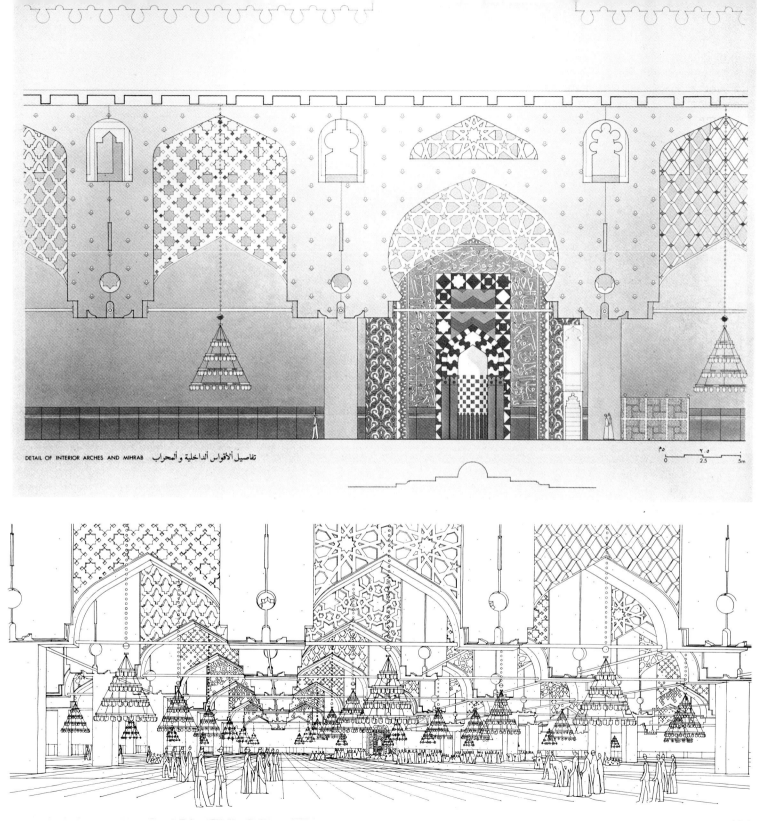

DETAIL OF INTERIOR ARCHES AND MIHRAB   تفاصيل الأقواس الداخلية والمحراب

Westway Park Project, New York, 1980-1984

Robert Venturi, John Rauch, Clarke and Rapuano Inc. Associated Architects.
Architects in Charge: Frederic Schwartz, Eric Fiss, Ronald McCoy
Collaborators: Colin Cathart, Steven Izenour, James King, Perry Kulper, Corbett Lyon, John Reddick, Mark Schimmenti, Denise Scott Brown, Thomas Shay

This is a large scale urban design project creating a 97-acre river-edge park and new development areas extending four miles along the Hudson River in Manhattan. Venturi, Rauch and Scott Brown, in association with landscape architects Clarke & Rapuano Inc., is responsible for design and programming of the parks system, development of a new street system and other highway-related architectural elements such as ventilation buildings, tunnel portals, signage, lighting, and finishes.

This continous river-front park —part of the $2 billion transportation project constructing a subsurface 6-lane interstate highway on landfill on Manhattan's West Side— will reopen the waterfront to the people of Manhattan, create new vitality along the river and enhance the rich public environment of the individual neighborhoods as they interconnect with the Hudson River.

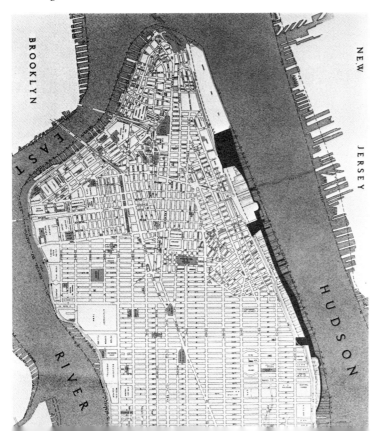

1. Lageplan in Manhattan
2. Fotomontage der Ansicht
3. Gesamtansicht des Modells

1. Site plan in Manhattan
2. Elevation photomontage
3. General view of the model

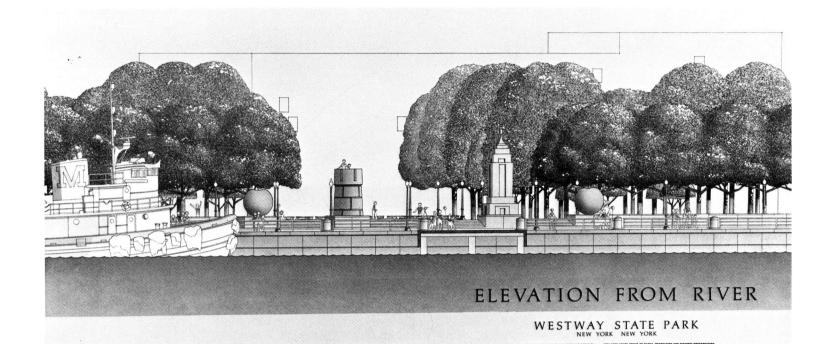

4. Ansicht vom Hudson River aus gesehen
5. Schnitt
6. Perspektive

4. Elevation from Hudson River
5. Section
6. Perspective

Ponte dell'Accademia, Biennale Venedig, 1985
Robert Venturi

Die Wettbewerbsunterlagen für den Entwurf des Ponte dell'Accademia aus dem Jahr 1843 besagten, daß die Entwurfsverfasser »angesehene Ingenieure« sein sollten. Die über hundertjährige bewegte Geschichte mit Vorschlägen und Änderungen zeigt, daß die Ingenieure, geachtet oder nicht, nicht gefeit waren gegen Konflikte und Widersprüche, hervorgerufen durch konstruktive Möglichkeiten, Kosten, Stil und öffentlichen Geschmack. Die Aufgabe ist demnach, so wie wir es sehen, eine reine Verschönerungsmaßnahme – um den Architekten, »die beschränkt waren auf den Entwurf der Ausschmückung«, eine Gelegenheit zu geben, genau dies zu tun.

Wir nehmen an, daß sich in hundertzweiundvierzig Jahren wenig verändert hat, und unsere Fähigkeit, einen öffentlichen Konsens zu erreichen darüber, wie die Dauerlösung für

Ponte Dell'Accademia, Venice Biennale, 1985
Robert Venturi

The competition brief for the Ponte Dell'Accademia of 1843 stated that the designers be limited to «reputable engineers». The subsequent checkered history of over a hundred years of proposals and alterations illustrates that engineers, reputable or not, were not immune from the conflicts and contradictions of structural efficiency, cost, style and public taste. The problem, then, as we see it, is a remedial one —to give the architects who were «relegated only to the design of the ornamentation» an opportunity to do just that.

We assume that little has changed in one hundred and forty-two years and our ability to arrive at a public consensus of what should be an appropriate permanent bridge is no better now than it was then. We recommend stabilizing and legitimizing the «temporary» wood and steel structure with the ad-

Gesamtansicht   General view

eine Brücke auszusehen hat, ist heute nicht größer als damals. Wir empfehlen, dem »Provisorium« aus Holz und Stahl durch Hinzufügen einer »dauerhaften« Schicht monumentaler, dekorativer, städtischer Symbole Festigkeit und Legitimation zu verleihen. Die von uns vorgeschlagenen Dekorationen erinnern an die Tradition der Cosmatenarbeiten und an die der venezianischen Marmorfassaden, wie die von S. Maria dei Miracoli und dem kleinen Palazzo Dario am Canal Grande.

Während die Muster traditionell sind, ist die Technik modern. Wir schlagen vor, eine Reihe von vorfabrizierten gegossenen Fiberglas-Paneelen mit Stahlwinkeln und Klammern an der bestehenden Konstruktion zu befestigen. Diese hohlen, verstärkten Paneele sind sehr leicht, so daß sie die Konstruktion nicht belasten. Jedes Paneel ist wasserundurchlässig beschichtet und sieht entweder aus wie Marmor oder, im Alternativentwurf, wie ein »Großmutter-Blumenmuster«.

dition of a «permanent» layer of monumental decorative civic symbolism. Our proposed decorative additions recall the tradition of Cosmati ornamentation and that of Venetian marble façades like those of S. Maria dei Miracoli and the diminutive Palazzo Dario on the Grand Canal.

While the patterns are traditional the technology is modern. We are proposing to hang a series of prefabricated molded fiberglas panels supported by steel angles and clips attached to the existing structure. These hollow reinforced panels are very light in weight so as not to compromise the structure. Each panel is coated with an impervious gel coat with integral color to simulate the marble patterns or, as in the alternate design, the «Grandmother's flower pattern».

Our interim solution to the complex evolution of the «temporary» Ponte Dell'Accademia is to add yet another layer of history and decoration in plastic to the existing layers of wood and steel.

Alessi Teeservice, 1981–1985
Robert Venturi
Mitarbeiter: James Bradberry, Denise Scott Brown, Maurice Weintraub

Das für Alessi entworfene silberne Teeservice besteht aus Kaffeekanne, Teekanne, Sahnekännchen, Zuckerdose und Tablett. Jedes Teil ist eine Reminiszenz an einen anderen historischen Stil, abstrahiert und symbolisiert durch Muster, die auf die silberne Oberfläche aufgebracht wurden. Die eklektische Symbolik erweckt reichhaltige und vieldeutige Assoziationen mit der dekorativen Kunst verschiedener Epochen.

Sekretäre für ARC International, 1984–1985
Robert Venturi
Mitarbeiter: Layng Pew, Maurice Weintraub
Foto: Matt Wargo

Diese drei Sekretäre wurden für ARC im Queen Anne-, Louis XV- und Louis XVI-Stil entworfen. Ihre historische Symbolik ist natürlich nicht wörtlich – die Art, wie sie abstrahiert ist, versucht, die Essenz jedes dieser konventionellen Stilrichtungen zu vermitteln. Und dieser abstrahierte (allerdings nicht abstrakte) Entwurf ist flächig, nicht dreidimensional; er ist das, was wir als gegenständlich bezeichnen – das ist eine Beschreibung, kein Ausdruck – ein Zeichen, wie die falsche Fassade eines Ladens auf dem Land. Auf diese Weise proklamieren wir eindeutig unser Ornament als symbolisch, nicht als substantiell und unsere Technik als modern und nicht als handwerklich. Das Fehlen von Reliefs gleichen wir aus durch gewagte Farben. Die Maßstäbe der Tische sind auch sehr kühn, so daß diese kleinen Stücke Präsenz haben.

Alessi Tea Service, 1981-1985
Robert Venturi
Collaborators: James Bradberry, Denise Scott Brown, Maurice Weintraub

The silver tea service designed for Officina Alessi includes a coffee pot, teapot, creamer, sugar bowl, and tray. Each piece is reminiscent of a different historical style abstracted and symbolized through various patterns applied to the silver surfaces. The eclectic symbolism provokes rich and ambiguous associations to decorative arts from different eras.

Bureaus for ARC International, 1984-1985
Robert Venturi
Collaborators: Layng Pew, Maurice Weintraub
Photography: Matt Wargo

These three bureaus designed for Arc are in the styles of Queen Anne, Louis XV, and Louis XVI. Their historical symbolism, of course, is not literal —it is abstracted in a way that attempts to convey the essence of each of these conventional styles. And this abstracted (not abstract, mind you) design is flat, not three-dimensional; it is what we call representational —that is, a depiction, not an expression— a sign like a false front on a country store. In this way, we unambiguously proclaim our ornament as symbolic, not substantive —also our technique as modern, not craft-like. We make up for the lack of relief by the boldness of the color. The scale is bold too, so these little pieces have presence.

Kaffee- und Teeservice — View of the coffee and tea set

Ansicht der Sekretäre — View of the tables

Möbelentwurf für Knoll International, 1979–1984

Robert Venturi

Mitarbeiter: Frederic Schwartz, Maurice Weintraub, Paul Muller, Denise Scott Brown

Die von Knoll in Auftrag gegebenen neuen Möbel umfassen neun Stühle aus Sperrholz, ein Sofa, einen Kaffeetisch und zwei hohe Tische. Diese Möbelstücke durchbrechen die Grenze zwischen traditionellem und modernem Design, da sie eine Reihe historischer Stilelemente auf industrielle Herstellungsverfahren anwenden und Symbolik und Dekoration in einer modernen Weise verarbeiten.

Die Stühle sind »sowohl-als-auch«, denn sie vereinen moderne Technologie mit historischer Symbolik, Komfort mit Eleganz, Funktion mit Witz. Von vorne betrachtet weisen sie eine komplexe Silhouette und eine von Ornamenten durchbrochene Oberfläche auf. Ohne die grundsätzliche Produktionsweise zu verändern, können die Muster enorm variiert werden. Daher können sie alles sein, von Chippendale bis Art Deco, eindimensional dargestellt. Die Oberfläche ist bei einigen Stühlen holzgemasert, bei anderen kunststoffbeschichtet in einheitlichen Farben. Bei wieder anderen ist die Beschichtung gemustert.

Bei allen Möbeln werden die Bezüge symbolisch und gegenständlich verwendet und nicht historisch getreu. Sie sollen als Exempel und Darstellung gelten, nicht als Reproduktion. Die historische Darstellung geschieht in Form eines Bildes aus einem Stil; das Betrachterauge soll nicht getäuscht werden. Das Profil der Möbelstücke ist abstrahiert und verallgemeinert, um die Silhouette herauszuheben.

Obwohl alle zur gleichen Zeit von einem Büro entworfen wurden, haben die Möbel kein einheitliches Motiv – aber sie sind einheitlich eklektisch.

Furniture Design for Knoll International, 1979-1984

Robert Venturi

Collaborators: Frederic Schwartz, Maurice Weintraub, Paul Muller, Denise Scott Brown

The new furniture commissioned by Knoll includes a series of nine laminated plywood chairs, a sofa, coffee table, and two high tables. This furniture breaks the boundary between traditional and Modern design by adapting a series of historical styles to industrial processes and by using symbolism and decoration in a Modern way.

The chairs are «both-and», combining modern technology with historic symbolism, comfort with elegance, function with fun. From the front view, they present a complex silhouette and a surface that is ornamentally perforated. The patterns may vary enormously without altering the basic method of production, therefore, they can be anything from Chippendale to Art Deco represented in one dimension. The surfaces of some of the chairs use wood grain, others have plastic laminate finishes in plain colors. Yet others are decorated with patterns within the laminate.

In all the furniture, the referents are used symbolically and representationally, not historically accurate. The aim is exemplification and representation, not reproduction. The historic representation is a picture of a style, it is not intended to fool the eye. The profile is abstracted and generalized to stress silhouette.

Although it was designed by one firm all at one time, this line of furniture has no motival unity —but it does have an eclectic unity. Its historical eclecticism, achieved through the representation of many styles, is paralleled by eclecticism of form and method. This furniture can be seen as part of the tradition of Modern furniture, as an evolution within the bounds of Modern design.

Verschiedene Stühle (Foto: Mikio Sekita, mit freundlicher Genehmigung von Knoll International)

View of several chairs (photo: Mikio Sekita, by courtesy of Knoll International)

Verschiedene Tische (Foto: Mikio Sekita, mit freundlicher Genehmigung von Knoll International)

View of circular tables (photo: Mikio Sekita, by courtesy of Knoll International)

Chronologie   Arbeiten und Projekte

1957 Haus Pearson, Chestnut Hill, Pennsylvania. Projekt.
1959 Renovierung des James B. Duke, Institut der Schönen Künste, New York.
Strandhaus. Projekt.
1960 Verwaltungszentrale der Vereinigung der ambulanten Krankenschwestern, Philadelphia.
Haus D. L. Miller, East Hampton, Long Island, New York.
Wettbewerb für ein F.D.R. Denkmal, Washington; mit G. Patton und N. Gianopulos.
1962 Grand's Restaurant, Philadelphia.
Haus Meiss, Princeton, New Jersey. Projekt.
Haus Vanna Venturi, Chestnut Hill, Pennsylvania.
1963 Haus Zinzer, Woodbury, Connecticut.
1964 Wettbewerb für einen Brunnen, Fairmount Park Association, Philadelphia; mit Denise Scott Brown.
1965 Guild House, Wohnhaus für ältere Menschen, Philadelphia; mit Cope & Lippincott.
Footlighters Theater, Pennsylvania; mit Paoli. Projekt.
Renovierung und Erweiterung des Allgemeinen Krankenhauses von Philadelphia.
Erweiterung des Hauses F. Otto Haas, Ambler, Pennsylvania.
1966 Eingangsgebäude, Mausoleum und Gedenkturm, Princeton Memorial Park, New Jersey. Projekt.
Wettbewerb für den Copley Square, Boston; mit G. Clark und A. Jones.
1967 Kulturzentrum Y.M.C.A., Ohio, Projekt.
Rathaus, Ohio, Projekt.
Bibliothekserweiterung, Ohio, Projekt.
Entwurf für die Neugestaltung der Hennepin Avenue, Minneapolis.
1968 Bürogebäude für Transportation Square, Washington; mit Laudell, Rowlett & Scott. Projekt.
Studie zur Neugestaltung von Hot Springs, Arcansas.
Haus N. Lieb, Long Beach Island, New Jersey.
Doppeljochige Feuerwache, Columbus, Indiana.
Hall of Fame des American Football. Projekt.
Entwurf für den Wiederaufbau der South Street, Philadelphia.
1969 Umgestaltung der St. Francis de Sales Kirche, Philadelphia.
1970 Büro-, Handels- und Theatergebäude für den Times Square, New York.
Generalplan für California City.
Wettbewerb für die Renovierung und Erweiterung der Mathematischen Fakultät, Yale University, New Haven. Erster Preis.
1971 Entwurf für die Wiederherstellung des Lawton Plaza, New Rochelle, New York. Projekt.
1972 Lagergebäude für BATO Papier-Gesellschaft, Greenwich, Connecticut.
Umbauentwurf für ein Konvent-Zentrum, Niagara Falls, Ontario.
1973 Einwohnerschafts- und Gemeindeeinkaufszentrum für Saga Harbour, Miami, Florida. Projekt.

Geisteswissenschaftliche Fakultät, Purchase, State University New York.
Gesundheitszentrum für das südöstliche Philadelphia; mit W. Mann. Projekt.
Wohnungsbau, Washington Square, Philadelphia. Projekt.
Trubek und Wislocki Häuser, Nantucket Island, Massachusetts.
Entwurf für die Zweihundertjahrfeier auf und um Benjamin Franklin Parkway, Philadelphia.
1974 Dixwell Feuerwache, New Haven, Connecticut.
Naturwissenschaftliches Museum, Roanoke, Virginia. Projekt.
Haus K. Cusak, Sea Isle City, New Jersey.
Haus Brant, Greenwich, Connecticut.
1975 C. Tucker House, Mount Kisco, New York.
Gemeindezentrum für das Marinekommando, Philadelphia Naval Base.
1976 Franklin Court, Restaurierung von fünf Häusern und Museum, Philadelphia.
Fakultätsclub für Pennsylvania State University.
Unterrichtsgebäude für Morris Arboretum, Philadelphia. Projekt.
Haus Brant, Vail, Colorado.
Erweiterung und Renovierung des Allen Memorial Art Museum für das Oberlin College, Ohio.
»Lebenszeichen: Symbole in der amerikanischen Stadt«, eine Ausstellung für die Renwick Galerie, Washington.
»200 Jahre amerikanische Skulpturen«, Installation für das Whitney Museum of American Art, New York City.
»Philadelphia: Drei Jahrhunderte amerikanische Kunst«, Installationsentwurf für die zweihundertjährige Ausstellung für Philadelphia Museum of Art.
1977 Ausstellungsgebäude für BASCO, Inc., Concord, Delaware.
Renovierung und Erweiterung des Marlborough-Blenheim Hotels, Atlantic City, New Jersey. Projekt.
Haus Brant, Bermuda.
Vorschlag für die Wiederbelebung von Main Street und The Hollow, Boonton, New Jersey.
Zeichen für das zentrale Geschäftsviertel von Salem, Massachusetts.
1978 Konservatorische Abteilung des Philadelphia Museum of Art.
Gebäude für Sozialwissenschaften, College von Purchase, State University of New York.
Entwicklungs- und Planstudie für Old City, Philadelphia.
»Mensch, Land und Umwelt«, Ausstellung für das Armee Ingenieur-Korps, Savannah District.
1979 Wettbewerb für den Pavillon der Vereinigten Staaten für die Internationale Energiemesse, Nashville, Tennessee.
Wettbewerb für das australische Parlamentsgebäude in Canberra, Erster Preis.
Verwaltungszentrale für das Institut für Wissenschaftliche Information, Philadelphia.
Entwurf für die Außenfassade für Best Products, Oxford Valley, Pennsylvania.

Ausstellungsraum und Konferenzraum für die Geschäftsleitung von Knoll International, New York.
1980 Wettbewerb für die Erweiterung des Museums für Kunsthandwerk, Frankfurt, Deutschland, Zweiter Preis.
Büroräume für Venturi, Rauch und Scott Brown, Philadelphia.
Bürogebäude, Montgomery Township, New Jersey.
Wettbewerb für einen 13000 m² großen Ausstellungskomplex für die Frankfurter Messe, Frankfurt, Deutschland.
Western Sector Plaza, Pennsylvania Avenue, Washington, D.C.; mit G. F. Patton.
1981 Erweiterung und Renovierung der Carroll Newman Bibliothek, Virginia Polytechnic Institute und State University; mit Vosbeck, Kendrick und Redinger.
Renovierung und Erweiterung der Settlement Musikschule, Philadelphia.
Restaurierung und Renovierung der Houston Hall, University of Pennsylvania, Philadelphia.
Hennepin Avenue, Minneapolis, Minnesota.
Gesamtplan für die Neugestaltung und Ausdehnung des Philadelphia Kunstmuseums.
»Zeitgenössischer Amerikanischer Realismus seit 1960«, Installation und Darstellungen für die Akademie der Schönen Künste, Pennsylvania.
1982 Appartementhaus mit 81 Wohnungen, Park Regency, Houston, Texas.
1983 Wettbewerb für die Staatsmoschee in Bagdad, Irak.
Welcome Park, Philadelphia.
Umbau des YMCA-Gebäudes in Philadelphia in 120 Appartements. Projekt.
Gordon Wu Hall, Butler College und Änderungen der Wilcox Hall, Princeton University.
Renovierung der Blair Hall und Commons Hall der Princeton University. Projekt.
1984 Laguna Gloria Kunstmuseum, Austin, Texas. Projekt.
Einkaufs-, Büro- und Wohnkomplex für Amanat Al Assima, Bagdad, Irak. Projekt.
Restaurierung und Wiedernutzbarmachung des Antilopenhauses, Zoologischer Garten von Philadelphia.
Einrichtung für Primaten, Zoologischer Garten von Philadelphia.
Gebäude für Molekularbiologie, Princeton University.
Stühle für Knoll International, New York.
Sekretäre für ARC International.
Westway Park, New York. Projekt.
Vorschläge für den Times Square, New York.
1985 Ponte dell'Accademia, Biennale Venedig. Ausgezeichnet mit dem Stone Lion.
Wohnhaus in East Hampton, New York.
Renovierung der Furness Library, University of Pennsylvania, Philadelphia.
Sunshine Foundation Feriencamp für chronisch kranke Kinder, Orlando, Florida.
Erweiterung des Reading Terminal Market, Philadelphia.
Anbau an die National Gallery, London, England.

Chronology. Works and Projects

1957 Pearson House, Chestnut Hill, Pennsylvania. Project.

1959 Renovations of the James B. Duke, Institute of Fine Arst. New York.
Beach House. Project.

1960 Headquarters Building, North Penn Visiting Nurse Association. Philadelphia.
D.L. Miller House, East Hampton, Long Island, New York.
F.D.R. Memorial Competition. Washington; with G. Patton and N. Gianopulos.

1962 Grand's Restaurant, Philadelphia.
Meiss House. Princeton, New Jersey. Project.
Vanna Venturi House. Chestnut Hill, Pennsylvania.

1963 Zinzer House. Woodbury, Connecticut.

1964 Fountain Competition, Fairmount Park Association. Philadelphia; with Denise Scott Brown.

1965 Guild House, Friends Housing for the Elderly. Philadelphia; with Cope & Lippincott.
Footlighters Theatre. Pennsylvania, with Paoli. Project.
Philadelphia General Hospital renovations and additions.
F. Otto Haas House additions. Ambler, Pennsylvania.

1966 Entrace Building, Mausoleum and Memorial Tower, Princeton Memorial Park. New Jersey. Project.
Copley Square Competition. Boston; with G. Clark and A. Jones.

1967 Comunity Centre Y.M.C.A. Ohio. Project.
City Hall. Ohio. Project.
Library addition. Ohio. Project.
Renewal plan for Hennepin Avenue. Minneapolis.

1968 Transportation Square Office Building. Washington; with Laudell, Rowlett & Scott. Project.
Renewal feasibility study of Hot Springs. Arcansas.
N. Lieb House. Long Beach Island, New Jersey.
Two-Bay Fire Station. Columbus, Indiana.
Hall of Fame of American Football. Project.
Rehabilitation plan for South Street. Philadelphia.

1969 St. Francis de Sales Church renovation. Philadelphia.

1970 Office, Commercial and Theatre Complex for Times Square. New York.
Master plan of California City.
Competition for the renovation and addition to the Mathematics Building, Yale University. New Haven. First Prize.

1971 Lawton Plaza redevelopment plan. New Rochelle, New York. Project.

1972 BATO paper Company Warehouse. Greenwich, Connecticut.
Convention Centre conversion plan. Niagara Falls, Ontario.

1973 Prototypical neighborhood and community shopping centers for Saga Harbour. Miami, Florida. Project.
Humanities Classroom Building, College at Purchase, State Universtity of New York.
Neighborhood health center for the Southeast Philadelphia; with W. Mann. Project.
Housing, Washington Square. Philadelphia. Project.
Trubek and Wislocki Houses. Nantucket Island, Massachusetts.
Design of the Bicentennial celebration on and around Benjamin Franklin Parkway. Philadelphia.

1974 Dixwell Fire Station, New Haven, Connecticut.
Natural Science Museum. Roanoke, Virginia. Project.
K. Cusak House, Sea Isle City, New Jersey.
Brant House. Greenwich, Connecticut.

1975 C. Tucker House. Mount Kisco, New York.
Community Center Building for the Naval Facilities Command. Philadelphia Naval Base.

1976 Franklin Court, restoration of five houses and Interpretative Museum. Philadelphia.
Faculty Club for Pennsylvania State University.
Educational Facility for Morris Arboretum. Philadelphia. Project.
Brant House. Vail, Colorado.
Additin and renovation of the Allen Memorial Art Museum for Oberlin College, Ohio.
«Signs of Life: Symbols in American City», an exhibition for the Renwick Gallery. Washington.
«200 Years of American Sculpture», instalation for the Whitney Museum of American Art, New York City.
«Philadelphia: Three Centuries of American Art», instalation design of the Bicentennial exhibition for the Philadelphia Museum of Art.

1977 Catalogue-Showroom for BASCO, Inc. Concord, Delaware.
Marlborough-Blenheim Hotel renovation and additions. Atlantic City, New Jersey. Project.
Brant House, Bermuda.
Proposal for the rejuvenation of Main Street and The Hollow. Boonton, New Jersey.
Signs for the central business district of Salem. Massachusetts.

1978 Conservation Laboratory for Philadelphia Museum of Art.
Social Sciences Buildings, College at Purchase. State University of New York.
Development and planning study for Old City. Philadelphia.
«Man, Land, and Environment», exhibition for the Army Corps of Engineers, Savannah District.

1979 Competition for the United States Pavilion at the International Exposition on Energy. Nashville, Tenessee.
Competition for the Australian Parliament House in Camberra. First Prize.
Headquarters Office Building for the Institute for Scientific Information. Philadelphia.
Exterior façade design for Best Products. Oxford Valley, Pennsylvania.
Showroom and executive Conference Room for Knoll International. New York.

1980 Competition for the addition to the Museum for Kunsthandwerk. Frankfurt, Germany. Second Prize.
Offices for Venturi, Rauch and Scott Brown. Philadelphia.
Office Building, Montgomery Township. New Jersey.
Competition for a 1.400.000 s.f. exhibition complex for the Frankfurther Messe. Frankfurt, Germany.
Western Sector Plaza, Pennsylvania Avenue. Washington, D.C.; with G.F. Patton.

1981 Addition and Renovation of the Carroll Newman Library, Virginia Polytechnic Institute and State University, with Vosbeck, Kendrick and Redinger.
Renovation and addition to the Settlement Music School. Philadelphia.
Restauration and renovation of Houston Hall, University of Pennsylvania. Philadelphia.
Hennepin Avenue. Minneapolis, Minnesota.
Master planning for the reorganization and expansion of the Philadelphia Museum of Art.
«Contemporary American Realism since 1960», instalation and graphics for the Pennsylvania Academy of Fine Arts.

1982 81 unit condominium, Park Regency. Houston, Texas.

1983 Competition for the State Mosque in Baghdad. Iraq.
Wellcome Park. Philadelphia.
Conversion of the Philadelphia YMCA building to 120 apartments. Project.
Gordon Wu Hall, Butler College and alterations to Wilcox Hall, Princeton University.
Renovation of Blair Hall and Commons Hall at Princeton University. Project.

1984 Laguna Gloria Art Museum. Austin, Texas. Project.
Retail, Office and Residential Building for Amanat Al Assima. Baghdad, Iraq. Project.
Restoration and reuse of Antelope House. Philadelphia Zoological Gardens.
New Primate exhibition facility. Philadelphia Zoological Gardens.
Molecular Biology Building at Princeton University.
Chairs for Knoll International. New York.
Bureaus for ARC International.
Westway Park. New York. Project.
Proposal for Times Square. New York.

1985 Ponte dell'Accademia, Venice Bienale. Awarded Stone Lion.
Residence in East Hampton, New York.
Renovation of Furness Library, University of Pennsylvania, Philadelphia.
Sunshine Foundation vacation campus for terminally ill children, Orlando, Florida.
Reading Terminal Market expansion, Philadelphia.
Extention to the National Gallery, London, England.

Biographien

Robert Venturi wurde 1925 in Philadelphia geboren und studierte Architektur an der Universität von Princeton. Von 1950–1958 arbeitete er für O. Stonorov, Eero Saarinen und L. I. Kahn. Er war Mitglied der Amerikanischen Akademie in Rom und lehrte an den Universitäten von Pennsylvania und Yale.

John Rauch wurde 1930 in Philadelphia geboren, studierte Architektur an der Universität von Pennsylvania, ist Leutnant der Amerikanischen Armee. Seine Partnerschaft mit R. Venturi besteht seit 1964. Innerhalb des Büros ist er für das Management verantwortlich.

Denise Scott Brown wurde in Südafrika geboren und studierte an der Architectural Association in London. Seit 1960 Zusammenarbeit mit R. Venturi bei theoretischen Arbeiten. Sie ist seit 1967 in dem Büro und dort verantwortlich für Stadtplanung und städtebauliche Projekte.

Biographies

Robert Venturi was born in Philadelphia in 1925 and studied architecture at Princeton University. From 1950 to 1958 worked for O. Stonorov, Eero Saarinen and L. I. Kahn. Has been fellow of the American Academy in Rome and has taught at Pennsylvania and Yale Universities.

John Rauch was born in Philadelphia in 1930, studied architecture at Pennsylvania University, is Lieutennant of the American Army and partner with R. Venturi since 1964. Is the management responsable for the works of the firm.

Denise Scott Brown was born is South Africa and studied at the Architectural Association in London. Since 1960 has collaborated with R. Venturi in theoretical projects. Joined the firm in 1967 and is responsable for the urban and urban planning projects.

Ausgewählte Bibliographie

A. Schriften über Venturi, Rauch und Scott Brown.

Stern, Robert A. M., *40 under 40,* Architectural League of New York, 1966 (Katalog zu einer Ausstellung in den Räumen der Architectural League von New York).
McCoy, Esther, »Buildings in the United States«, in: *Lotus,* Bd. 4, 1967/8, SS. 15–123.
Goldberger, Paul, »Less is More – Mies van der Rohe. Less is Bore – Robert Venturi«, in: *The New York Times Magazine,* 19. Oktober 1971, SS. 24–37 ff.
»Venturi and Rauch«, in: *L'Architecture d'Aujourd'hui,* Dezember 1971–Januar 1972, SS. 84–104.
Miguel, Pere Ferrero, »Brown, D. S. y Venturi, R., ›Aprendiendo de todas las cosas‹«, in *ABC* (Madrid), 26. April 1972.
»Venturi and Rauch 1970–74«, in: *Architecture and Urbanism* (Japan), November 1974 (Monographie über das Werk Venturis und Rauchs).
Dixon, John Morris, Hrsg., »Venturi and Rauch«, in: *Progressive Architecture,* October 1977, SS. 49–69. (Artikel über das Werk des Büros von John Dixon, Stuart Cohen, Martin Filer, David Morton und Suzanne Stephens).
von Moos, Stanislaus, Hrsg., »Venturi and Rauch: 25 Public Buildings«, in: *Werk-Archithese,* Juli–August 1977, SS. 2–64 (Monographie über das Büro).
Dunster, David, Hrsg., »Venturi and Rauch« in: *Architectural Monographs 1,* London Academy Editions, 1978 (Monographie über das Büro).
Nakamura, Toshio, Hrsg., »Recent Works by Venturi and Rauch«, in: *Architecture and Urbanism,* Januar 1978, SS. 2–80 (Monographie über das Büro).
»Venturi, Rauch and Scott Brown«, in: *Summarios,* Mai 1979 (Monographie über das Büro).
Pain, Richard, »Venturi and Rauch. House in Delaware: Vernacular Layering. A Thematic Analysis«, in: *International Architect,* Nr. 9/Bd. 2, Ausgabe 1/1982, SS. 7–18.
Schmertz, Mildred F., »Learning from Denise: The Role in Architecture of DSB«, in: *Architectural Record,* Juli 1982, SS. 102–107.
Wines, James, »Setting the Record Straight: The Work of Venturi, Rauch and Scott Brown«, in: *Express,* Herbst 1982, SS. 12–13.
Chimacoff, Alan und Plattus, Alan, »Learning from Venturi«, in: *Architectural Record,* Sept. 1983-II.
Mateo, Josep-Lluis, Dir., *Quaderns,* 162 (1984) (Monographie über das Büro).
Bletter, Rosemarie Haag, »Transformation of the American Vernacular: The Work of Venturi, Rauch & Scott Brown«, in: *Venturi, Rauch and Scott Brown: A Generation of Architecture,* Ausstellungskatalog, März 1984, SS. 2–19.
Grabar, Oleg, »From the Past into the Future: On Two Designs for State Mosque«, in: *Architectural Record,* Juni 1984, SS. 150–151.

B. Schriften von Robert Venturi

»The Campidoglio: A Case Study« in: The *Architectural Review,* Mai 1953, SS. 333–334.
Complexity and Contradiction in Architecture. New York: Museum of Modern Art, 1966; Zweite Auflage 1977. (Auch in französisch, spanisch, deutsch, griechisch, italienisch, japanisch und serbokroatisch erschienen).
»A Bill-Ding Board Involving Movies, Relics and Space«, in: *Architectural Forum,* April 1968, SS. 74–76.
»Complexity and Contradiction in the Work of Furness«, in: *Pennsylvania Academy of the Fine Arts Newsletter,* Frühjahr 1976, S. 5.
»Plain and Fancy Architecture by Cass Gilbert at Oberlin and the Addition to the Museum by Venturi and Rauch«, in: *Allen Memorial Art Museum Bulletin,* Bd. 34, Nr. 2, 1976–77, SS. 83–104. (Ebenfalls erschienen in: *Architectura,* Januar–Februar 1978, SS. 66–74. Ein Teil dieses Artikels erschien in: *Apollo,* Februar 1976, SS. 6–9).
»Alvar Aalto«, in: *Arkkitehti,* Juli–August 1976, SS. 66–67. (Nachgedruckt in: *Progressive Architecture,* April 1977, SS. 54, 102.)
»A Definition of Architecture as Shelter with Decoration on It, and Another Plea for a Symbolism of the Ordinary in Architecture«, in: *Architecture and Urbanism,* Januar 1978, SS. 3–14. (Ebenfalls erschienen in: *L'Architecture d'Aujourd'hui,* Nr. 197, Juni 1978, SS. 7–8.)
»Learning the Right Lessons from the Beaux Arts«, in: *Architectural Design,* Januar 1979, SS. 23–31.
»Il Proprio Vocabolario«, in: *Gran Bazaar,* Februar 1982, SS. 152–157. (Artikel über das Haus Brant. Siehe auch Rezension »Venturi, Rauch and Scott Brown«, S. 43.)
»RIBA Discourse, July 1981«, Transactions 1, in: *RIBA Journal,* Mai 1982, SS. 47–56.
»Diversity, Relevance and Representation in Historicism, or Plus ça Change ... plus A Plea For Pattern all over Architecture with a Postscript on my Mother's House«, in: *Architectural Record,* Juni 1982, SS. 114–119. (Ebenfalls erschienen in: *L'Architecture d'Aujourd'hui,* Oktober 1982, SS. 94–101 und in: *Arquitecturas,* 3/1984, SS. 24–29.)
»On Aalto«, in: *Quaderns 157,* April, Mai, Juni 1983, S. 55.
»Proposals for the Iraq State Mosque, Baghdad«, in: *L'Architecture d'Aujourd'hui,* Sept. 1983, SS. 28–35.

C. Schriften von Denise Scott Brown

»Form, Design and the City«, in: *Journal of the American Institute of Planners,* November 1962.
»The Meaningful City«, in: *Journal of the American Institute of Architects,* Januar 1965, SS. 27–32. (Nachgedruckt in: *Connection,* Frühjahr 1967.)
»The Function of a Table«, in: *Architectural Design,* April 1967.
»Housing 1863«, in: *Journal of the American Insitute of Planners.* Mai 1967.

»Planning the Powder Room«, in: *Journal of the American Institute of Architects,* April 1967, SS. 81–83.

»Teaching Architectural History«, in: *Arts and Architecture,* Mai 1967.

»Team 10, Perspecta 10, and the Present State of Architectural Theory«, in: *Journal of the American Institute of Planners,* Januar 1967, SS. 42–50.

»The Bicentennials's Fantasy Stage«, in: *The Philadelphia Evening Bulletin,* 8. März 1968.

»Mapping the City: Symbols and Systems«, in: *Landscape,* Frühjahr 1968, SS. 22–25.

»Urban Structuring«, in *Architectural Design,* Januar 1968, S. 7.

»Urbino«, in: *Journal of the American Institute of Planners,* September 1968, SS. 344–346

»Learning from Pop«, und »Reply to Frampton«, in: *Casabella,* 389/390, Mai–Juni 1971, SS. 14–46. (Nachgedruckt in: *Journal of Popular Culture,* Herbst 1973, SS. 387–401.)

»A House is More than a Home« (mit Steven Izenour, Dian Boone, Missy Maxwell, Robert Venturi, Elizabeth Izenour und Janet Schueren), in: *Progressive Architecture,* August 1976, SS. 62–67.

»On Architectural Formalism and Social Concern: A Discourse for Social Planners and Radical Chic Architects«, in: *Oppositions 5,* Sommer 1976, SS. 99–112.

Signs of Life: Symbols in the American City (mit Steven Izenour). New York: Aperture, Nr. 77, 1976, SS. 49–65 (Ausstellungskatalog).

»Suburbane Space, Scale and Symbol« (mit Elizabeth Izenour, Missy Maxwell und Janet Schueren), in: *Via,* University of Pennsylvania, 1976.

»Forum: The Beaux Arts Exhibition«, in: *Oppositions,* Frühjahr 1977, SS. 165–166.

»Learning the Wrong Lessons from the Beaux-Arts«, in: *Architectural Design,* Profiles 17, 1979, SS. 30–32.

»Architectural Taste in a Pluralistic Society«, in: *The Harvard Architecture Review,* Bd. 1, Frühjahr 1980, SS. 41–51.

»Between Three Stools: A Personal View of Urban Design Practice and Pedagogy«, in: *Education for Urban Design,* SS. 132–172, Purchase, NY: Institute for Urban Design, 1982.

»Drawing for the Deco District«, in: *Archithese,* 2-82, 4. März 1982, SS. 17–21.

»The Drawings of Buildings«, für die Ausstellung »Building and Drawings, Venturi, Rauch and Scott Brown«, Max Protetch Galerie, New York, 1982.

»Invention and Tradition in the Making of American Place«, Skript für eine Konferenz mit dem Titel »American Architecture: Innovation and Tradition«, April 1983. Wird noch veröffentlicht.

»A Worm's Eye of Recent Architectural History«, in: *Architectural Record,* Februar 1984, SS. 69–81.

»Visions of the Future Based on Lessons from the Past«, in: *Center,* Bd. 1, 1985, SS. 44–63.

D. Schriften von Robert Venturi und Denise Scott Brown

»Learning from Lutyens«, in: *Journal of the Royal Institute of British Architects,* August 1969, SS. 353–354.

»Mass Communications on the People Freeway, or, Piranesi is Too Easy«, in: *Perspecta* 12, 1969, SS. 49–56.

»Some Houses of Ill-Repute: a Discourse with Apologia on Recent Houses of Venturi and Rauch«, in: *Perspecta,* 13/14, 1971, SS. 259–267.

»Ugly and Ordinary Architecture, or the Decorated Shed«, Teil 1, in: *Architectural Forum,* November 1971, SS. 64–67; Teil II, Dezember 1971, SS. 48–53.

Learning from Las Vegas (mit Steven Izenour). Cambridge, Mass.: MIT Press, 1972, zweite Auflage 1977. (Auch in französisch, spanisch, deutsch und japanisch erschienen.)

»Functionalism, Yes, But…«, in: *Architecture and Urbanism,* November 1974, SS. 33–34. (Ebenfalls erschienen in: *Architecturas Bis,* Januar 1975, SS. 1–2; und in: *Werk-Archithese,* März 1977, SS. 32–35.)

»Interview, Robert Venturi and Denise Scott Brown«, in: *The Harvard Architecture Review,* Bd. 1, Frühjahr 1980, SS. 228–239.

A View from the Campidoglio: Selected Essays, 1953–1984, New York: Harper & Row, 1984.

Interview mit Robert Venturi und Denise Scott Brown, geführt von Barbaralee Diamonstein für: *American Architecture Now II.* New York: Rizzoli, 1985.

E. Schriften von Denise Scott Brown und Robert Venturi

»On Ducks and Decoration«, in: *Architecture Canada,* Oktober 1968, S. 48.

»The Bicentennial Commemoration 1976«, in: *Architectural Forum,* Oktober 1969, SS. 66–69.

Aprendiendo de Todas Las Cosas. Barcelona: Tusquets Editor, 1971.

Bibliography

A. Writings about Venturi, Rauch and Scott Brown

Stern, Robert A. M., *40 under 40,* Architectural League of New York, 1966. (Catalog for exhibit at the Architectural League of New York).

McCoy, Esther, «Buildings in the United States», *Lotus,* vol. 4, 1967/8, pp. 15-123.

Goldberger, Paul, «Less is More — Mies van der Rohe. Less is a Bore — Robert Venturi», *The New York Times Magazine,* October 19, 1971, pp. 24-37ff.

«Venturi and Rauch», *L'Architecture d'Aujourd'hui,* December 1971-January 1972, pp. 84-104.

Miguel, Pere Ferrero, «Brown, D.S., y Venturi, R.; 'Aprendiendo de todas las cosas'», *ABC* (Madrid), April 26, 1972.

«Venturi and Rauch 1970-74», *Architecture and Urbanism* (Japan), November 1974. (Monograph on the work of Venturi and Rauch).

Dixon, John Morris, ed., «Venturi and Rauch», *Progressive Architecture,* October 1977, pp. 49-69. (Articles on the work of the firm by John Dixon, Stuart Cohen, Martin Filer, David Morton, and Suzanne Stephens).

von Moos, Stanislaus, ed., «Venturi and Rauch: 25 Public Buildings», *Werk-Archithese,* July-August 1977, pp. 2-64. (Monograph on the firm).

Dunster, David, ed., «Venturi and Rauch», *Architectural Monographs 1.* London: Academy Editions, 1978. (Monograph on the firm).

Nakamura, Toshio, ed., «Recent Works by Venturi and Rauch», *Architecture and Urbanism,* January 1978, pp. 2-80. (Monograph on the firm).

«Venturi, Rauch and Scott Brown», *Summarios,* May 1979. (Monograph on the firm).

Pain, Richard, «Venturi and Rauch. House in Delaware: Vernacular Layering. A Thematic Analysis», *International Architect,* N.° 9/Vol. 2: Issue 1/1982, pp. 7-18.

Schmertz, Mildred F., «Learning from Denise: The Role in Architecture of DSB», *Architectural Record,* July 1982, pp. 102-107.

Wines, James, «Setting the Record Straight: The Work of Venturi, Rauch and Scott Brown», *Express,* Fall 1982, pp. 12-13.

Chimacoff, Alan and Plattus, Alan, «Learning from Venturi», *Architectural Record,* Sept. 1983-II.

Mateo, Josep-Lluís, dir., *Quaderns,* 162 (1984). (Monograph on the firm).

Bletter, Rosemarie Haag, «Transformations of the American Vernacular: The Work of Venturi, Rauch & Scott Brown», *Venturi, Rauch and Scott Brown: A Generation of Architecture,* Exhibition Catalog, March 1984, pp. 2-19.

Grabar, Oleg, «From the Past into the Future: On Two Designs for State Mosques», *Arquitectural Record*, June 1984, pp. 150-151.

B. Writings by Robert Venturi

«The Campidoglio: A Case Study», *The Architectural Review*, May 1953, pp. 333-334.

Complexity and Contradiction in Architecture. New York: Museum of Modern Art, 1966; second edition 1977. (Also published in French, Spanish, German, Greek, Italian, Japanese, and Serbo-Croatian).

«A Bill-Ding Board Involving Movies, Relics and Space», *Architectural Forum*, April 1968, pp. 74-76.

«Complexity and Contradiction in the Work of Furness», *Pennsylvania Academy of the Fine Arts Newsletter*, Spring 1976, p. 5.

«Plain and Fancy Architecture by Cass Gilbert at Oberlin and the Addition to the Museum by Venturi and Rauch», *Allen Memorial Art Museum Bulletin*, Vol. 34, N.° 2, 1976-77, pp. 83-104. (Also in *Architectura*, January-February 1978, pp. 66-74. A portion of this article appeared in *Apollo*, February 1976, pp. 6-9).

«Alvar Aalto», *Arkkitehti*, July-August 1976, pp. 66-67. (Reprinted in *Progressive Architecture*, April 1977, pp. 54, 102).

«A Definition of Architecture as Shelter with Decoration on It, and Another Plea for a Symbolism of the Ordinary in Architecture», *Architecture and Urbanism*, January 1978, pp. 3-14. (Also in *L'Architecture d'Aujourd'hui*, N.° 197, June 1978, pp. 7-8).

«Learning the Right Lessons from the Beaux Arts», *Architectural Design*, January 1979, pp. 23-31.

«Il Proprio Vocabolario», *Gran Bazaar*, February 1982, pp. 152-157. (Article on Brant Houses. See also review, «Venturi, Rauch and Scott Brown», p. 43).

«RIBA Discourse, July 1981», Transactions 1, *RIBA Journal*, May 1982, pp. 47-56.

«Diversity, Relevance and Representation in Historicism, or Plus ça Change... plus A Plea For Pattern all over Architecture with a Postcript on my Mother's House», *Architectural Record*, June 1982, pp. 114-119. (Also in *L'Architecture d'Aujourd'hui*, October 1982, pp. 94-101; *Arquitecturas*, 3 1984, pp. 24-29).

«On Aalto», *Quaderns 157*, April, May, June 1983, p. 55.

«Proposal for the Iraq State Mosque, Baghdad», *L'Architecture d'Aujourd'hui*, Sept. 1983, pp. 28-35.

C. Writings by Denise Scott Brown

«Form, Design and the City», *Journal of the American Institute of Planners*, November 1962.

«The Meaningful City», *Journal of the American Institute of Architects*, January 1965, pp. 27-32. (Reprinted in *Connection*, Spring 1967).

«The function of a Table», *Architectural Design*, April 1967.

«Housing 1863», *Journal of the American Institute of Planners*. May 1967.

«Planning the Powder Room», *Journal of the American Institute of Architects*, April 1967, pp. 81-83.

«Teaching Architectural History», *Arts and Architecture*, May 1967.

«Team 10, Perspecta 10, and the Present State of Architectural Theory», *Journal of the American Institute of Planners*, January 1967, pp. 42-50.

«The Bicentennial's Fantasy Stage», *The Philadelphia Evening Bulletin*, March 8, 1968.

«Mapping the City: Symbols and Systems», *Landscape*, Spring 1968, pp. 22-25.

«Urban Structuring», *Architectural Design*, January 1968, p. 7.

«Urbino», *Journal of the American Intitute of Planners*, September 1968, pp. 344-346.

«Learning from Pop», and «Reply to Frampton», *Casabella*, 389/390, May-June 1971, pp. 14-46. (Reprinted in *Journal of Popular Culture*, Fall 1973, pp. 387-401).

«A House is More than a Home» (with Steven Izenour, Dian Boone, Missy Maxwell, Robert Venturi, Elizabeth Izenour, and Janet Schueren), *Progressive Architecture*, August 1976, pp. 62-67.

«On Architectural Formalism and Social Concern: A Discourse for Social Planners and Radical Chic Architects», *Opositions 5*, Summer 1976, pp. 99-112.

Signs of Life: Symbols in the American City (with Steven Izenour). New York: Aperture, N.° 77, 1976, pp. 49-65. (Exhibition catalog).

«Suburban Space, Scale and Symbol» (with Elizabeth Izenour, Missy Maxwell, and Janet Schueren), *Via*, University of Pennsylvania, 1976.

«Forum: The Beaux Arts Exhibition», *Oppositions*, Spring 1977, pp. 165-166.

«Learning the Wrong Lessons from the Beaux-Arts», *Architectural Design*, Profiles 17, 1979, pp. 30-32.

«Architectural Taste in a Pluralistic Society», *The Harvard Architecture Review*, Vol. 1, Spring 1980, pp. 41-51.

«Between Three Stools: A Personal View of Urban Design Practice and Pedagogy», *Education for Urban Design*, pp. 132-172. Purchase, NY: Institute for Urban Design, 1982.

«Drawing for the Deco District», *Archithese*, 2-82, March 4, 1982, pp. 17-21.

«The Drawings of Buildings», for the exhibition, «Building and Drawings, Venturi, Rauch and Scott Brown», Max Protetch Gallery, New York, 1982.

«Invention and Tradition in the Making of American Place», paper for a conference «American Architecture: Innovation and Tradition», April 1983. To be published.

«A Worm's Eye of Recent Architectural History», *Architectural Record*, Feb. 1984, pp. 69-81.

«Visions of the Future Based on Lessons from the Past», *Center*, Vol. 1, 1985, pp. 44-63.

D. Writings by Robert Venturi and Denise Scott Brown

«Learning from Lutyens», *Journal of the Royal Institute of British Architects*, August 1969, pp. 353-354.

«Mass Communications on the People Freeway, or, Piranesi is Too Easy», *Perspecta 12*, 1969, pp. 49-56.

«Some Houses of Ill-Repute: a Discourse with Apologia on Recent Houses of Venturi and Rauch», *Perspecta 13/14*, 1971, pp. 259-267.

«Ugly and Ordinary Architecture, or the Decorated Shed», Part I, *Architectural Forum*, November 1971, pp. 64-67; Part II, December 1971, pp. 48-53.

Learning from Las Vegas (with Steven Izenour). Cambridge, Mass.: MIT Press, 1972, second edition 1977. (Also published in French, Spanish and Japanese)

«Functionalism, Yes, But...» in *Architecture and Urbanism*, November 1974, pp. 33-34. (Also in *Arquitecturas Bis*, January 1975, pp. 1-2; *Werk-Archithese*, March 1977, pp. 32-35

«Interview, Robert Venturi and Denise Scott Brown», *The Harvard Architecture Review*, Vol. 1, Spring 1980, pp. 228-239.

A View from the Campidoglio: Selected Essays, 1953-1984, New York: Harper & Row, 1984.

Robert Venturi and Denise Scott Brown interviewed by Barbaralee Diamonstein for *American Architecture Now II*. New York: Rizzoli, 1985.

E. Writings by Denise Scott Brown and Robert Venturi

«On Ducks and Decoration», *Architecture Canada*, October 1968, p. 48.

«The Bicentennial Commemoration 1976». *Architectural Forum*, October 1969, pp. 66-69.

Aprendiendo de Todas Las Cosas. Barcelona: Tusquets Editor, 1971.